Mathematics in Educa

CW00687180

Delivering Curriculum Pathways
in
Mathematics

2005

This paper was compiled and published in May 2005 by Mathematics in Education and Industry (MEI).

ISBN: 0948 186 17 8

To order more copies or for further information about this paper:
email *office@mei.org.uk*
or visit *www.mei.org.uk*.

Typeset in 11 pt Palatino Linotype.
Printed and bound in Great Britain by Heron Press, Westbury, Wiltshire.

Contents

Preface vii

About the authors viii

Executive summary ix

Part A: **Background** 1

1 **Rationale** 1
  1.1   Introduction 1
  1.2   Overseas comparisons 2

2 **Unsolved problems** 3
  2.1   Qualifications at age 16 3
  2.2   Take-up post-16 5

3 **Assessment issues** 6
  3.1   Should examinations be age related? 6
  3.2   What does grading represent? 7
  3.3   Assessment for mastery 7
  3.4   Assessment of desired outcomes 8

Part B: **A pathways model** 9

4 **Student profiles** 9
  4.1   Illustrating students' progress 9
  4.2   Interpreting the student profiles 11
  4.3   Commentary on the student profiles 11

5 **Designing a qualifications framework** 12

6 **Pathways** 14
  6.1   Routes of progression 14
  6.2   The general design 15
  6.3   Some previous fixed level frameworks (pre-16) 16

Part C: **Relating the pathways model to our mathematics curriculum**   **17**

7   **Comparison with present qualifications**   **17**

7.1   Approximate equivalence   17

7.2   Major differences from the present provision   17

7.3   Naming the elements   18

7.4   The new pathways   19

7.5   Assessment of the new elements   21

8   **Changes to GCSE qualifications**   **22**

8.1   The element GCSE1   22

8.2   The element GCSE2   25

8.3   The relationship between GCSE1 and GCSE2   26

8.4   Functional Mathematics   27

8.5   The relationship between difficulty and uptake   30

8.6   A framework for improved provision   31

9   **Take-up post-16**   **32**

9.1   Students are discouraged by GCSE   32

9.2   Lack of suitable courses   32

9.3   Mathematics is perceived to be harder than other subjects   34

10   **Looking after the needs of all**   **35**

10.1   Entry Level and Level 1 provision   35

10.2   Talented students   37

11   **Comparison with the Smith report**   **38**

11.1   Comparison with the Smith recommendations   38

11.2   Comparisons with pathways models in the Smith report   42

11.3   The Tomlinson report   46

Part D: The way ahead   47

12   **How the pathways model supports the White Paper**   47
              12.1   Entry Level and Level 1   47
              12.2   GCSE   47
              12.3   AS and A Level Mathematics   48
              12.4   Further Mathematics   50
              12.5   Other mathematics courses for Year 12 and 13 students   50
              12.6   Making use of ICT   51

13   **Development work needed**   53

14   **Integrity**   54
              14.1   Entry Level and Level 1   54
              14.2   Acceleration   55
              14.3   Assessment for mastery   57
              14.4   Delivery   58

Conclusion   59

Appendix: Problem solving   61

              Case study: Is mathematical development supported
              through a problem solving curriculum?   61
              Problem solving and mathematical thinking   65

References and notes   67

Preface

This paper follows on from the publication of *Making Mathematics Count*, the report of Professor Adrian Smith's Inquiry into Post-14 Mathematics Education in February 2004, and the subsequent government White Paper, *14–19 Education and Skills*, published in February 2005. The White Paper also drew on the findings of *14–19 Curriculum and Qualifications Reform*, the October 2004 report, covering all subjects, of the 14–19 Working Group chaired by Mike Tomlinson. In this paper quotations from the Smith report are printed in blue; those from the White Paper are in red.

The Smith report may be seen as inviting a search for a better curriculum structure for mathematics in England for ages 14 to 19, one in which there is a coherent set of pathways for young people to follow. This paper, which was commissioned by the QCA, is written as a serious contribution to that search.

The paper has been compiled and published by Mathematics in Education and Industry (MEI) but the team responsible for it covers a much wider spectrum of the mathematics community than a single organisation.

It is written in four parts.
- Part A is devoted to background issues.
- In Part B a pathways model is developed from first principles, based upon the reality of students' profiles of attainment.
- In Part C this model is compared to the present curriculum structure.
- Part D looks ahead, detailing how the proposed model matches with the plans in the White Paper and the development work that will be necessary; the final chapter looks at important issues that have come to the surface.

The particular model recommended in this paper fits in with our wider curriculum of GCSEs, A Levels and vocational qualifications. However, the underlying analysis is based on students' needs and attainment profiles rather than any particular examination structure, and so the model could validly be refined to meet a different set of curriculum requirements.

Roger Porkess　　　　　　*David Holland*
Tandi Clausen-May　　　　　　*Jane Imrie*
Paul Dickinson　　　　　　*Michael Ling*
Frank Eade　　　　　　*Bernard Murphy*
Doug French　　　　　　*Jenny Piggott*
Gerald Goodall　　　　　　*Charlie Stripp*

March 2005

About the authors

Roger Porkess is Chief Executive of MEI. As well as writing much of this paper he compiled the contributions from the whole team.

Tandi Clausen-May is a Principal Research Officer at the National Foundation for Educational Research (NFER); for 8 of the last 12 years she has been a General Council Member of the Association of Teachers of Mathematics (ATM).

Paul Dickinson is a Lecturer at the Centre for Mathematics Education at Manchester Metropolitan University.

Frank Eade is a Lecturer at the Centre for Mathematics Education at Manchester Metropolitan University.

Doug French is a Lecturer in Education at the University of Hull and is President Designate of the Mathematical Association (MA).

Gerald Goodall is Director of Education and Professional Affairs at the Royal Statistical Society (RSS).

David Holland is Deputy Chairman of MEI and a senior examiner at A Level.

Jane Imrie is a consultant at the Standards Unit of the DfES where she is Teaching and Learning Project Manager – Mathematics.

Michael Ling is Professional Support Officer for MEI and a senior examiner and coursework moderator.

Bernard Murphy is the Programme Leader for the Teaching Advanced Mathematics project, run by MEI.

Jenny Piggott is Director of the NRICH Mathematics Project, based at the University of Cambridge.

Charlie Stripp is the Programme Leader for the Further Mathematics Network, run by MEI, and is Chairman of the Teaching Committee of the Mathematical Association (MA).

Executive summary

- In this paper a new set of pathways for 14–19 mathematics are developed.

- The pathways are consistent with the government's recent White Paper and with the recommendations of the Smith Inquiry.

- These pathways will ensure a much better provision for our young people, and so a higher level of engagement with the subject.

- The pathways are designed to meet the needs and aspirations of all learners, not just those towards the middle of the spectrum.

- Qualifications will be based on definite standards, rather than being age related, ensuring that they will be meaningful to end-users.

- There will be a double award at GCSE, mirroring the provision of Mathematics and Further Mathematics at A Level.

- The problems related to tiering at GCSE will disappear, so that every student entering the examinations has the possibility of obtaining a grade C (or better).

- The grade thresholds for GCSE qualifications will be significantly higher than at present.

- A qualification in Functional Mathematics will be available for those who do not attain the first GCSE.

- The design avoids the need to divide children into 'haves' and 'have-nots' at the age of 14; the problems associated with O Level and CSE will not resurface.

- Routes of progression will be available post-16 for those taking mathematics as a subject in its own right and for those taking it as a service subject.

- Many more students can be expected to continue with mathematics post-16.

Part A: Background

1   Rationale

1.1   Introduction

In February 2005, the government published a White Paper entitled *14–19 Education and Skills*[1]. This followed the earlier publication of two reports in 2004, *Making Mathematics Count* from the Post-14 Mathematics Inquiry[2] (the Smith report) in March and *14–19 Curriculum and Qualifications Reform* from the Working Group on 14–19 Reform[3,4] (the Tomlinson report) in October.

The Smith report recognised that there are problems with our present mathematics curriculum and the different pathways through it. In Recommendation 4.11, it called for studies of a number of pathway models. This paper presents one such model and relates it to the relevant recommendations of the Smith report and the subsequent White Paper (which subsumes the Tomlinson report). The starting point for the model is the actual performance profiles of students in our schools and colleges.

It would be true to say that there has been considerable unease over our national mathematics provision in recent years. A symptom of this has been the frequent changes; for example in the last 12 years there have been 4 different A Level regimes and a similar number at GCSE. The Smith recommendation for study of further models indicates a belief that these changes have still failed to address the problems.

So before developing any new model, it is important to look below the surface and ask whether there are underlying structural issues that need to be addressed. Two such deep-seated problems are identified in Chapter 2. Both of them may well be described as unsolved problems, in that we have never in our history come close to dealing with them.

There are also problem areas where known solutions are not being implemented effectively. Meeting the needs of students at either extreme of the distribution of ability and using appropriate assessment instruments are two examples. These are addressed in the course of this paper.

1.2 Overseas comparisons

The fact that other countries do not seem to share our problems might seem to give credence to the view that, if we look overseas, we will find solutions. However, differences between our education system and those of other countries mean that this is not in fact the case.

In most countries students continue with a broad range of subjects, including mathematics, to the age of 18. England is unusual in requiring specialisation at 16, and in the extent of that specialisation. A consequence of specialisation at 16 is the need for an external examination at that age, leading to certification in those subjects that students will then drop. Thus GCSE presents a much more significant hurdle to our students than is the case with assessment at 16 in most countries.

In addition, we need to be aware of cultural differences. In some of the most successful countries in international studies, mathematics has long been regarded as one of the good things in life.

So, although there is much we can learn from looking at systems in other countries (see, for example, the section in the Appendix about problem solving in Holland), we will not find a curriculum that can be taken off the shelf and used here. In Section 11.2 the Swedish curriculum, presented in the Smith report, is shown to be inappropriate for our situation. The only way that we will have a successful curriculum is if we design it ourselves, to meet our particular circumstances.

2   Unsolved problems

2.1   Qualifications at age 16

England has never had a satisfactory mathematics curriculum for the full cohort of students at the age of 16.

Until comparatively recently, many children were expected to have left school before they were 16. The minority who did stay on used to take School Certificate; in 1950 that was replaced by O Level.

School attendance patterns began to change significantly after the Second World War with increasing numbers staying on beyond the age of compulsory schooling, culminating in Raising of the School Leaving Age in 1973–4.

Many of those staying on in the 1950s and 1960s were found to be less than well suited to O Level and so new CSE courses were devised in most subjects, including mathematics. The first CSE examinations were sat as early as 1962, well before Raising of the School Leaving Age. CSE courses were intended to be innovative and attractive, bringing a level of education to children who had previously been denied it.

A CSE grade 1 was supposed to be equivalent to an O Level pass (at one time grade 6 but later grade C). However, many end-users, particularly employers, were sceptical about the equivalence and showed a marked preference for O Level over CSE. Consequently, children who chose to do CSE courses, or more commonly were allocated to them, were seen as second rate. The decision about which course was to be followed was usually made at the age of 14 and many children (and their parents) were very resentful of what they saw as a labelling process.

The introduction of GCSE in 1986–8, combining CSE and O Level into a single examination, was designed to rectify the situation. However, it has not proved successful as far as end-users are concerned. Those entering employment are perceived not to have the skills they need, and the same criticism is made of those continuing mathematics as a sixth form subject. These concerns are well documented; the following example is taken from the opening paragraph of the General Conclusions in the report *Mathematical Skills in the Workplace*[5].

> *… mathematical skills in the workplace are changing, with increasing numbers of people involved in mathematics-related work, and with such work involving increasingly sophisticated mathematical activities. In agreement with other recent studies, we conclude that the country needs to rethink and look to upgrade mathematics provision for young people and to ensure that people have access to additional provision over their lifetimes.*

Whether by coincidence or not, since the introduction of GCSE, the number of students taking A Level Mathematics has declined substantially.

There was initially some variety in the style of GCSE syllabuses. However, from 1997 all GCSE syllabuses were subject to new regulations, resulting in fewer and less distinctive syllabuses.

One of the major problems with GCSE Mathematics is that it is expected to cover the full range of students' attainment at the age of 16. Research has shown that among 16-year-olds the range of mathematical development covers 10 years[6]; even without the upper and lower 20% tails, it is still about 6 years. Thus a GCSE in Mathematics does not, and cannot, represent any particular standard. However, the expectation of end-users is that it should do just that.

In attempts to resolve the tension between measuring students' attainment across this wide range and providing a certificate that will be valued by end-users, a number of different tiering arrangements have been tried. None has been successful; solving one problem creates another.

With a large number of tiers, many weaker students find themselves entered for a tier where the papers are appropriate for them but their possible grades are restricted; thus a Foundation Tier candidate on the present 3-tier system has a ceiling of grade D, which is widely regarded as a failure. This has proved to be very de-motivating.

However, with fewer tiers the papers have to cover wider ranges. This has two negative affects: the lowest grade on a paper is often awarded on a very low mark, and syllabus coverage can only be achieved with more, shorter questions and so less emphasis can be placed on the fundamental mathematical skill of problem solving.

In summary, we have had four systems in England.

- School Certificate
- O Level
- O Level and CSE
- GCSE

Major problems have been associated with all of them.

There never was a Golden Age. There have been times when we have met the needs of our more able children at the age of 16, but we have never had a satisfactory provision for the whole cohort. The proposals in this paper set out a curriculum structure which is designed to do so for the very first time.

2.2 Take-up post-16

The provision post-16 has also failed to adapt to the needs of a much wider range of students. When A Levels began in 1951, only a small minority of young people stayed in education post-16. The proportion staying on now is very much greater but, in the absence of suitable pathways, not many of them do any mathematics.

Thus, whereas in many countries virtually all young people stay in education post-16 and continue with mathematics, in England and Wales less than 10% of the age cohort take mathematics post-16. The main reasons for such a small take-up include the following.

- Students are discouraged in mathematics by their experience in GCSE.
- There is a lack of suitable courses.
- Mathematics is perceived to be harder than other subjects at A Level.

Clearly we have a national problem. It is true that we have had a higher take-up rate in the not too distant past but it has never been more than 20%, nowhere near that in most other industrialised countries.

At this age, too, we have failed to adapt our mathematics curriculum to the need to educate more than a small group of the most able students each year. It is not just that many more students should be taking AS and A Level, true though that is, but that we fail to provide suitable mathematics for those engaged in vocational courses.

3   Assessment issues

3.1   Should examinations be age related?

The current mathematics curriculum may be described as being pivoted on GCSE. With only a few exceptions, GCSE is the focus for pre-16 courses and the starting point for those for use post-16.

In paragraph 4.1 the Smith report identified many of the problems with the current GCSE arrangements. It also acknowledged the proposal in the interim Tomlinson report to move away from age related qualifications.

> *The interim report includes proposals to move away from the existing age-related qualifications to a system offering more opportunities for students to achieve qualifications in their own time and at their own ability and aptitude level, while offering coherent pathways of progression.*

This was reiterated in Recommendation 2 of the final Tomlinson report.

> *Young people should be able to enter the framework at age 14 at the level that best meets their capabilities and complete more than one diploma as they progress through the 14–19 phase.*

The Smith report did not really explore the issues that this proposal raises. Instead it made the more general Recommendation 4.11 that there should be a number of studies into possible pathways. However, it is taken up in the White Paper, for example in the final bullet point on page 44.

> *We will challenge and support schools to ensure that young people take qualifications when they are ready, ending 16 as a fixed point in the system …*

The model described in this paper is based upon the assumption that examinations need not necessarily be age related.

Other subjects in which examinations are not age related included music, with grades running from 1 through to 8, taken when a learner is ready, and more recently the Asset scheme for modern languages[7].

The implications of early entry for schools are discussed in Sections 14.2.1, 14.4.1 and 14.4.2.

3.2   What does grading represent?

In most qualifications a better grade is awarded for a better performance on essentially the same assessment of the same content. Thus in university finals, people sit the same papers and, according to their marks, are awarded a class of degree: 1, 2-1, 2-2, 3, Ordinary (etc.).

That, however, is not the case with GCSE Mathematics. Those who take different tiers sit different papers on substantially different syllabuses with essentially different grades available. Indeed someone who is awarded grade A has studied a completely different syllabus from someone with grade F. (See Section 14.3.1 for a more detailed explanation.)

Thus GCSE is not a single qualification but 3 essentially different qualifications, one for each tier, under the same title. Within any tier, a better grade is the result of a better performance, but between tiers different grades result from studying, in effect, different syllabuses.

There is thus a fundamental difference in the way that mathematics is graded at GCSE and at A Level. At A Level there are two subjects, Mathematics and Further Mathematics. The full range of grades is available on each. A candidate who takes both subjects has studied different syllabuses for each of them. The relationship between the two syllabuses has been carefully thought out, particularly for the new specifications where much of the early Further Mathematics work is a broadening of that undertaken in the single subject.

In the model to be described in this paper, GCSE will be graded in much the same way as A Level, with the full range of grades available on each of two separate awards. The pretence that the work covered by the present GCSE is the same for all is discontinued.

3.3   Assessment for mastery

A consequence of the need to cover a wide range of attainment in a limited number of papers is that very low thresholds are common in the present GCSE. On one paper in 2004, the grade C threshold was set at 14% and on another the grade B threshold was 17%.

Such low thresholds are extremely damaging to the external credibility of the qualification. What value is there in a certificate that effectively says its holder cannot do the work? They are also very destructive to students' self-confidence and so their willingness to continue the subject post-16. Furthermore they are technically unreliable since the outcome is based on candidates' performance on only a very few questions.

They are a consequence of a combination, on the one hand, of the association between syllabus content and grades, and on the other hand, of the need to assess a range of grades on the same paper. (See Section 14.3.1 for a more detailed explanation.) Many candidates find themselves taking papers on which most of the questions cover topics they have not learnt, a demoralising experience.

The same problem does not arise at A Level with target thresholds of 80% for grade A and 40% for grade E. All candidates should have met all the topics covered; discrimination is achieved through the difficulty built into the questions.

The White Paper does not take up the suggestion in the Tomlinson Report that A* and A** grades should be introduced at level 3 or, in this context, A Level. This would have placed pressure on the grading system and in time would probably have led to lower grade thresholds. Many candidates would have been faced with papers that appeared to be designed to find what they could not do, rather than to allow them to show what they could do.

3.4   Assessment of desired outcomes

There is currently a conflict between what is assessed in mathematics and the outcomes that are really desired. Several important skills, like problem solving, modelling and extended reasoning, are difficult to assess, and so tend to be treated lightly if at all. By contrast, it is easy to set examination questions on routine calculations and so this tends to happen.

Consequently much of the assessment, and the associated teaching effort, is not directed at the most desired outcomes, the deeper thinking that is required for problem solving.

Throughout this paper there is considerable emphasis on problem solving. Some associated issues are discussed in the Appendix; the implications for providing teachers with appropriate professional development are raised in Section 14.4.4.

Part B: A pathways model

4   Student profiles

4.1   Illustrating students' progress

A mathematics curriculum needs to take account of three variables:

(a)   students' level of attainment in mathematics
(b)   their mathematical ability
(c)   their age.

For a curriculum to be successful it has to be based on the relationship between all three of these variables. It is common practice to try to represent our curriculum and the associated pathways as a 2-dimensional diagram on a sheet of paper but this often leads to misrepresentation of what is essentially a 3-dimensional situation.

A familiar representation of a similar situation is provided by the growth curves to be found in any doctor's surgery. In these the horizontal axis represents Age and the vertical axis Height. The inherent variability between children is illustrated by different curves on the graph representing different percentiles through the range. Such a chart is reproduced at the end of this paper[29].

It would be possible to represent mathematical growth in the same way, but with Attainment rather than Height on the vertical axis. However, such a representation could, by analogy, be interpreted as meaning that at a certain age people stop learning mathematics (just as they stop growing), and that it is beyond their control to do anything about it. Rather than risk such misinterpretation, a different form of graph is used in this paper and this is illustrated in Figure 1 overleaf.

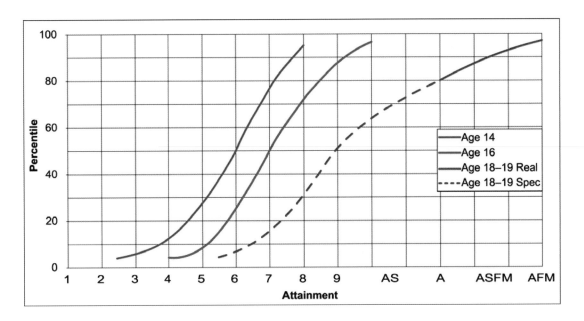

Figure 1:   The performance of our students

In this diagram the three variables are designated as follows.

4.1.1 Attainment

The horizontal axis represents Attainment. This is measured by National Curriculum Level (2 to 9), running on into AS and A Level Mathematics and then Further Mathematics.

The scale is approximately linear (but with some uncertainty, particularly around the transitions from GCSE to AS Level), although this is not actually essential to the analysis that follows.

4.1.2 Mathematical ability

The vertical axis represents Mathematical ability, measured by the percentile within the age cohort. It is a matter of observation that, within any class or age cohort, some students are consistently more successful in mathematics than others. This is no doubt a combination of a number of factors such as natural talent, work ethic and motivation.

It should be noted, however, that the ranking among students is not fixed over time; late developers, for example, tend to move up the scale as they get older.

4.1.3 Age

The third variable, Age, is represented by the three ogives, corresponding to ages 14, 16 and 18–19. (Further ogives could be drawn for other ages.) These three have been drawn using available data.

- The ogive for 14-year-olds is based on the published 2003 Key Stage 3 results[8] and so is accurate.
- That for age 16 is based on the published 2003 GCSE results[9]. These have been converted to National Curriculum levels using the accepted scale[10]. These include a small number of candidates of ages other than 16 and so the ogive may not be quite as accurate as that for age 14.
- Much of the ogive for ages 18–19 is speculative since in the current system most of that age group have given up mathematics anyway. However at the top it is based on AS and A Level experience and this part is shown with a continuous line.

4.2   Interpreting the student profiles

Within the limitations mentioned above, Figure 1 is fact. It represents what is actually happening in our schools and colleges.

Each horizontal line represents a particular percentile. The point where it crosses the ogives gives the attainment of those students at ages 14, 16 and 18–19. The three examples in the table below illustrate this for students who are (consistently) on the 80th, 50th and 20th percentiles.

Percentile	Age 14	Age 16	Age 18–19
80	7	8–9	A Level
50	6	7	Not reached AS
20	4–5	Nearly 6	7

4.3   Commentary on the student profiles

This description is not materially altered by any uncertainty about the precise positions of the ogives.

The close relationship between the ogives for 14- and 16-year-olds is interesting and, since the data sources used to construct them were independent, also reassuring.

They show the median student moving from Level 6 at the age of 14 to Level 7 at 16, giving an approximate equivalence of half a Level per year. Students on lower percentiles seem to progress at much the same rate, but those on higher percentiles progress somewhat faster.

At age 16 a student on the 95th percentile is at Level 10, one on the 5th percentile at Level 4, a gap of 6 Levels. This corresponds rather accurately with the 10-year gap found nearly 20 years earlier by Professor Margaret Brown[6].

5   Designing a qualifications framework

Since Figure 1 (on page 10) illustrates the performance of our students, it provides an authoritative basis on which to address the question '*What sort of framework of courses and qualifications do we need to meet the needs of students between the ages of 14 and 19?*'

A possible answer is illustrated in Figure 2, below, where a number of vertical lines have been added to Figure 1 to represent the maximum assessment levels for possible qualifications. These are equally spaced through the National Curriculum Levels; the spacing going on to M5 and M6 is somewhat wider.

In the rest of this document the term *element* is used to describe a course leading up to such an assessment, the assessment itself and any qualification that may ensue.

At this stage, these elements are denoted by M1, M2, M3, M4a, b and c, M5, M5c and M6. The use of these context-free titles indicates that up to this stage, the development could be described as being largely from first principles.

In Chapter 7, the various elements are related to current and possible future provision and given titles that are more easily recognised. They are described in more detail in Chapter 8 and subsequently, and they are related to the recommendations of the Smith report and the requirements of the White Paper.

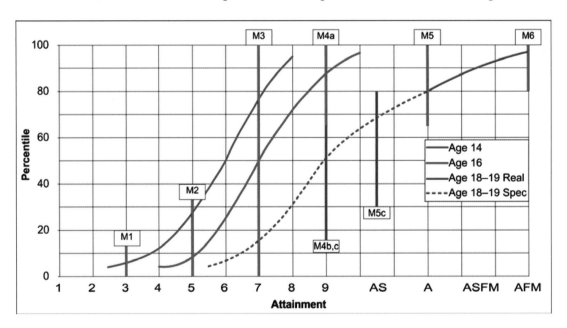

Figure 2: Assessment points

A number of principles have motivated this particular design.

- All qualifications should be tied to certain levels of attainment.
- There should be a basic qualification (M3) which almost everyone can aspire to attain, a passport for many aspects of adult life.
- The needs of students of all abilities must be met at all stages.
- Delivery must be feasible, despite the variety of types of school and college.

In practice, no mathematics assessment is based on a single standard. In an examination some short questions are designed to be easier than others; long questions start with easier parts and progress to harder ones. Often 'harder' means a somewhat higher attainment level within a topic.

The vertical lines in Figure 2 represent maximum assessment levels for the various elements. Possible ranges of levels are illustrated in Figure 3. It should, however, be stressed that this diagram illustrates the overall design; detailed development work will be needed to ensure it is used to best effect.

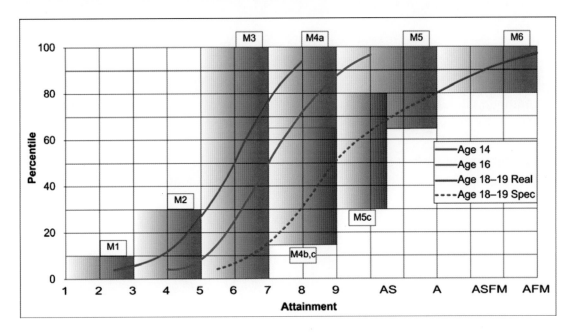

Figure 3: Assessment ranges

6   Pathways

6.1   Routes of progression

In Chapter 4, the progress of three students was tracked; they were on the 80th, 50th and 20th percentiles. The table below shows the elements that will be available to these students as they progress through their education, according to this design.

Percentile	Age 14	Age 16	Age 18–19
80	M3	M4a	M5
50	–	M3	M4b, M4c
20	–	M2	M3

The students on the 80th and 50th percentile are well served by the element M3 and the pathways leading on from it.

However, the student on the 20th percentile is only really ready for M3 when aged 18–19. Should this student leave education before that age, he or she would probably have no mathematics qualification at all if M3 were the only available qualification (in common with many of today's young people). The element M2 will meet the need of such a student for a more basic element to be taken at an earlier age (typically 16).

The pattern of Figure 2 (on page 12) would suggest that M2 could also be an element for middle-ranking students at the age of 14 (for example someone on the 50th percentile). However, it is the intention that this element should only be used by its target group, those who are not ready for M3 by the age of 16.

The design covers the full range of students, not just those between the 80th and 20th percentiles. Possible provision for those in the tails of the distribution is illustrated in the next table.

Percentile	Age 14	Age 16	Age 18–19
95	M3	M4a	M6
90	M3	M4a	M5–6
10	–	M2	M2–3
5	–	M1–2	M2

The various elements in this design fit together to form the complete set of pathways illustrated in Figure 4 overleaf.

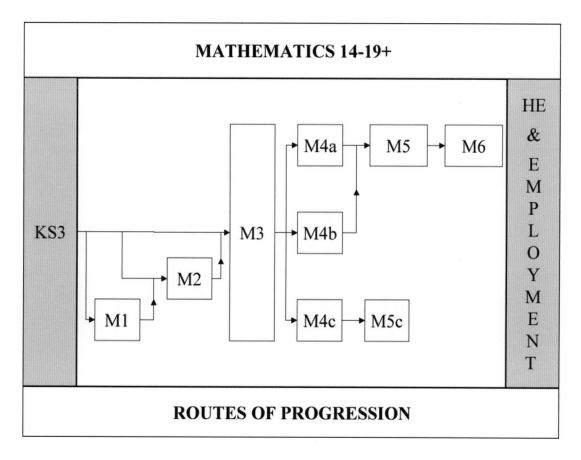

Figure 4: Pathways

6.2   The general design

The general design is a particular response to the pattern of student achievement illustrated in Figure 1 on page 10. The vertical lines, representing assessment points, could be drawn in different places, and there could be more or fewer of them. There are thus other possible similar designs within the same generic framework.

So far, the ideas have been developed as a theoretical model and for that reason the elements have been given the abstract names, M1, M2 and so on.

However, the decisions over where to place the assessment points were heavily influenced by present practice, and are broadly consistent with it. The White Paper states, on page 44,

> *We will retain GCSEs and A Levels as cornerstones of the new system.*

Consequently most of the elements can be described using terms in current use, like 'Entry Level' and 'A Level'. In Chapter 7, the various elements are matched to the present curriculum and at that point they are given working names.

6.3   Some previous fixed level frameworks (pre-16)

There have been earlier pre-16 curriculum frameworks based on fixed level assessment.

Graduated Assessment in Mathematics (GAIM) divided the curriculum into 15 levels (later reduced to 13) and provided extensive teaching material to cover all of them. The GAIM levels formed the basis for the 10 National Curriculum Levels.

The MEI National Curriculum scheme provided assessments from Level 4 to Level 10, which could be taken at any time. Students were awarded GCSE on the results of their 3 highest Level assessments.

Neither GAIM nor the MEI scheme survived the changes to GCSE in 1997, requiring exactly 3 tiers of entry.

6.3   Some previous fixed level frameworks (pre-16)

Part C: Relating the pathways model to our mathematics curriculum

7 Comparison with present qualifications

7.1 Approximate equivalence

The table below shows the approximate equivalence between the elements M1 to M6 and existing qualifications.

Element	Equivalent	Notes
M1	Entry Level	
M2	Foundation Tier GCSE	These 3 elements cover what is currently described by the single term GCSE. (There are also some FSMQs at these Levels.) However they will involve some different skills and M4a will extend the most able.
M3	Intermediate Tier GCSE	
M4a	Higher Tier GCSE	
M4b	VCE Units FSMQs	For post-16 students only
M4c	GCSE Statistics FSMQs	For post-16 students only
M5	A Level Mathematics	Including the current AS Mathematics and AS Use of Mathematics
M5c	AS Statistics	
M6	Further Mathematics	Including the current AS Further Mathematics

7.2 Major differences from the present provision

There are two areas where this framework differs significantly from the present provision, and these relate to the two unsolved problems identified in Chapter 2.

- Instead of being presented as a single entity, GCSE Mathematics is replaced by 3 elements of increasing depth, M2, M3 and M4a.
- There is an enhanced and much more coherent provision for students wishing to take some mathematics post-16, including those on vocational courses.

These differences are discussed in greater depth in Chapters 8 and 9.

The new requirement for Functional Mathematics will be incorporated into this framework (see Section 8.4).

7.3   Naming the elements

At this point in the development of the model it is appropriate to give the various elements working names with appropriate abbreviations. The figures in the second column are National Qualifications Framework levels.

Previous	Level	New working title	Abbreviation
M1	Entry	Entry Level Mathematics	Entry
M2	1	Level 1 Mathematics	L1
M3	2	GCSE Mathematics 1	GCSE1
M4a	2	GCSE Mathematics 2	GCSE2
M4b	2	Applicable Mathematics	AM
M4c	2	Statistics	S1
M5c	3	AS Statistics	S2
M5	3	AS and A Level Mathematics	A
M6	3	Further Mathematics	FM

In addition to these elements, there will be the national qualification in Functional Mathematics, as announced in the White Paper. Where appropriate, this is given the abbreviation Fn.

7.4   The new pathways

The new pathways are illustrated in Figure 5, below. This is an amended version of Figure 4 (see page 15).

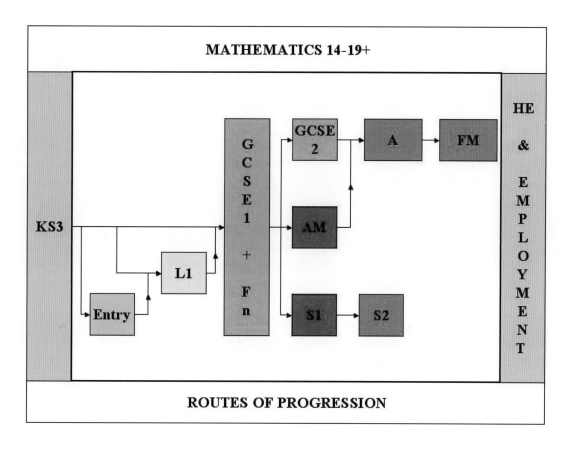

Figure 5: New pathways

Most students enter these pathways after Key Stage 3 at the end of Year 9. However, Figure 5 (together with the earlier Figure 4) needs to be interpreted with care since the representation is 2-dimensional. It could give the impression that all students leave Key Stage 3 at the same standard. The reality, as shown in Figure 1 (see page 10), is that there is a wide range of attainment at this point, from students who are well up to the standard of GCSE1 to others who have yet to reach National Curriculum Level 3.

Typical routes of progression from Key Stage 3 will be as follows.

- Some students will be ready to take GCSE1 at this point, or shortly afterwards, and will proceed to GCSE2, typically in two years time.

- Many students will begin a 2-year course aimed at GCSE1.

- The remaining students will start on Entry or Level 1 courses, either Entry + Level 1 Mathematics or Level 1 Mathematics only. Many of these will proceed to GCSE1 after completing the Level 1 qualification.

During Years 10 and 11, most students will spend the normal time allocation of 180 hours on mathematics. However, a possible effect of having two GCSE qualifications available is that some schools will increase the teaching time given to mathematics in Years 10 and 11, perhaps to over 200 hours.

In Years 10 and 11, the statutory requirements for those aged 14–16 will apply, so there will be no possibility of students giving up mathematics during this period.

The two post-16 Level 2 elements, Applicable Mathematics and Statistics, are expected to take target students (those who have successfully completed GCSE1 at the end of Year 11) roughly the equivalent of an AS unit, 60 Guided Learning Hours. However, both these units have yet to be designed and so it would be premature to judge this time; it could perhaps be that longer times turn out to be more appropriate.

The teaching time requirements for the A Level and Further Mathematics elements would be much the same as at present, about 360 Guided Learning Hours.

The element S2 will be the equivalent of an AS Level and so would require about 180 hours.

7.5   Assessment of the new elements

The levels of the assessments for the various elements are indicated in Figure 6 below. (This is based on Figure 3, see page 13, but updated to include the new names of the elements.)

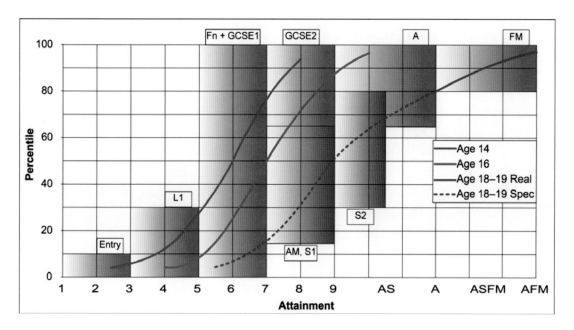

Figure 6: Assessment ranges for new elements

The assessment methods proposed for the Entry and Level 1 elements are described in Sections 10.1.1 and 10.1.2; those for GCSE1, GCSE2 and Functional Mathematics are covered in Sections 8.1.3, 8.2.3 and 8.4.4 respectively.

A Level and Further Mathematics will continue to be assessed on a modular basis but it is likely that the changes at GCSE will feed through, with more emphasis on problem solving and, possibly, the use of some on-line examinations.

No development work has yet taken place on the two new post-16 elements, currently entitled Applicable Mathematics and Statistics, but it seems likely that they will both require an examination and possibly some portfolio work or coursework.

The AS Statistics element will almost certainly involve modular examinations, with the possibility of additional portfolio work or coursework.

8   Changes to GCSE qualifications

In this framework, the present GCSE is replaced by three separate qualifications, Level 1 Mathematics, GCSE1 and GCSE2, corresponding broadly to Foundation, Intermediate and Higher Tiers. Compared with GCSE each of these covers a relatively narrow band of content (about 2 National Curriculum levels). The comparison is not, however, an exact one since the new elements will require a much greater emphasis on problem solving and thinking skills and will represent different levels of competence in these aspects.

The Level 1 element will not carry GCSE status (in contrast to Foundation Tier GCSE) but GCSE1 and GCSE2 will form the two Subjects in a double award GCSE. This is consistent with bullet point 3 on page 60 of the White Paper.

> *At GCSE we will continue work to reform maths as proposed by Professor Adrian Smith, improving motivation and progression to advanced level. This is likely to include a new double maths GCSE.*

In thinking about this double award, the analogy with A Level Mathematics and Further Mathematics will be found helpful. This will be particularly true at the design stage; the broadening nature of the new AS Further Mathematics, and the fact that it can be taken alongside the single A Level, may well be features that are transferable to the new GCSE qualifications.

These two GCSE elements, GCSE1 and GCSE2, will be key to the whole framework. Subsequent elements will follow on from them and the two earlier elements, Entry Level and Level 1 Mathematics, will be informed by GCSE1.

8.1   The element GCSE1

The element GCSE1 will serve several purposes.

- It will be the first part of a double subject GCSE qualification.
- Part of it will provide the national qualification in Functional Mathematics recommended in the White Paper.
- It will be a way-stage for more talented students going on to take more mathematics in its own right.
- It will also be a way-stage for students going on to take service mathematics courses in support of other subjects, both academic and vocational; such courses will not assume knowledge beyond GCSE1.

Meeting these different needs will involve careful design bringing together outcomes, content, assessment and pedagogy. Since the whole framework in this paper depends on getting this element right, its design has been the subject of quite considerable thought and this is summarised in the following subsections.

8.1.1 Outcomes

The intention is that GCSE1 will provide the basic national qualification in mathematics. Like the driving test, by far the majority of people will be expected to pass it sooner or later.

To be useful as a national qualification it must empower students to use mathematics confidently in their everyday lives, whether at work or in study. It must enable them to be functional in the subject.

8.1.2 Content

It is proposed that much of the mathematics in this element should be learnt in context, but that 'context' should be defined rather broadly as 'situations with which the students are comfortable'. According to this definition, on the one hand, contexts can be quite abstract but, on the other hand, would not usually involve everyday situations that are outside the students' experience.

Suitable notice would be taken of paragraph 4.20 in the Smith report.

> *The inquiry is acutely aware of the dangers of diluting the essence of the discipline of mathematics by inappropriate attempts to make everything immediately 'relevant' and by the use of clearly unrealistic versions of 'real' problems. That said, we believe that the time has come for a radical re-look at longer term options for 14–16 mathematics provision that do provide sufficient appropriate pathways for those who need motivating more through perceived practical relevance. We shall make recommendations directed at beginning this process. …*

8.1.3 Assessment

Two parts are proposed for the assessment of GCSE1, an on-line test and a written test of problem solving skills. The written test will be assessed externally.

The on-line test will be available on demand but it is suggested that a candidate will not be able to repeat a test until a suitable time, say 3 months, has elapsed. Considerable development work will be needed before it is possible to say just how this will work, but it may be that the tests will be generated randomly from a large, stratified bank of questions.

The on-line test could provide part or all of the assessment for the new qualification in Functional Mathematics, as described in paragraph 5.9 of the White Paper.

We will ensure that young people can gain a qualification for achieving the functional skills, even if they are not able to achieve a full GCSE. QCA should secure the development of alternative qualifications ... to be studied alongside the KS4 programmes of study. We expect, however, that most students should continue to complete a full GCSE.

The use of on-line assessment for this purpose is consistent with paragraph 10.13 in the White Paper.

E-assessment can also support our drive to improve functional English and maths. At present the questions are predominantly multiple choice, but we are working with QCA to expand the tests to examine a broader range of skills. We will ask QCA to draw on this experience in developing tests in functional skills as part of GCSE English and maths. This should include ensuring that they are available on-line and on-demand, both to support learning and to allow assessment as soon as the young person is ready.

It is proposed that passing the on-line assessment should be a pre-requisite for obtaining a GCSE grade C or above, as described in bullet point 5 on page 36 of the White Paper.

...we will ensure that no-one can get a grade C or better in English and maths without mastering the functional elements. Where a young person masters the functional elements only, we will recognise that separately.

It is also proposed that the grades from C up to A* would then be awarded on the basis of the written paper.

The relationship between GCSE1 and the national qualification in Functional Mathematics is discussed further in Section 8.4.4.

On-line tests will reduce the assessment burden described in both the Smith and Tomlinson reports but, in contrast to other forms of internal assessment, will not increase teachers' workload.

8.1.4 Pedagogy

The design of GCSE1 is expected to draw on existing research and development work.

An example is the work from the Freudenthal Institute of the University of Utrecht, in conjunction with the University of Wisconsin-Madison, resulting in the *Mathematics in Context* set of materials[11]. These materials are currently being used on a trial basis by some schools in the Manchester area under the supervision of Manchester Metropolitan University. This experience underlies the further discussion of the role of problem solving in the mathematics curriculum in the Appendix. The extent and quality of these materials demonstrate that it will be possible to devise a worthwhile GCSE1 qualification that will benefit virtually the whole ability range.

Teaching this element will place different demands upon teachers than, say, Intermediate Tier GCSE. They will need training in appropriate pedagogy. This will build upon and extend improvements in pedagogical practice that have come in with the National Strategy.

8.2   The element GCSE2

The element GCSE2 will form the second and more demanding part of the double award GCSE. It will also be consistent with the Smith Recommendation 4.5 for an extension curriculum and assessment framework. (This does, however, raise issues which are discussed further in Section 10.2.) Students taking GCSE2 will typically be among about the top 30–35% of the cohort and many will take the assessment at the age of 16.

8.2.1 Outcomes

This element will empower students to continue to study mainstream mathematics, providing them with appropriate thinking and problem solving skills as well as content knowledge and technical fluency.

8.2.2 Content

Its content will be guided by the current Higher Tier GCSE but not necessarily constrained by it.

8.2.3 Assessment

Three possible forms of assessment are envisaged. As for GCSE1, there will be an on-line test and a written examination covering problem solving skills. In addition there could be an extension paper using questions like those used for the National Mathematics Competition.

8.2.4 Pedagogy

The pedagogy required for this element will be based heavily on problem solving as well as mastery of techniques and so, while close to that needed for the new GCSE1, will be rather different from that currently employed by many teachers of Higher Tier GCSE.

8.3   The relationship between GCSE1 and GCSE2

There is a difference in the relationship between current Intermediate and Higher Tier GCSEs and that between the new Mathematics and Further Mathematics A Levels. This is illustrated in Figure 7. At GCSE, the Higher Tier follows on sequentially from the Intermediate and would best be described as a deepening of the content. By contrast at A Level, the early part of Further Mathematics is a broadening of the single AS and A Level, rather than necessarily a deepening.

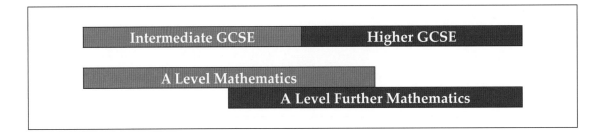

Figure 7: Contrasting assessment patterns

The new GCSEs would benefit from a relationship like that between Mathematics and Further Mathematics. It would make it easier for teachers to ensure that talented students are adequately stimulated when working for GCSE1. This is discussed further in Section 14.4.3.

8.4   Functional Mathematics

8.4.1 Requirements for Functional Mathematics

The Tomlinson report recommended that the cores of the various diplomas should include Functional Mathematics and this idea is taken up in the White Paper.

- Paragraph 7.2 of the White Paper describes a requirement for Functional Mathematics in the employer-designed diplomas.

  ... In order to complete any Diploma, a young person will need to demonstrate at the appropriate level:

  o   *a core of functional skills in English and maths;*

- Functional Mathematics is also to be a requirement in the context of GCSE, as stated in bullet point 5 of the summary to Chapter 5 of the White Paper.

  we will ensure that no-one can get a C or better in English or maths without mastering the functional elements. Where a young person achieves the functional element only, we will recognise that separately

- The point is taken further in the next bullet point.

  we will make sure that this functional core is the same in the adult Skills for Life qualifications, other Key Skills qualifications and in the GCSEs

8.4.2 The meaning of Functional Mathematics

Annex C of the final Tomlinson report left it for others to define the content of Functional Mathematics.

> *Content ... To be determined by QCA, actively seeking advice and views from experts and end-users.*

In the White Paper it is described in paragraph 5.5.

> *Functional English and maths are the English and maths that people need to participate effectively in everyday life, including in the workplace.*

The consultation process described in the Tomlinson report began with a conference organised by QCA and ACME on March 3rd 2005. In summary, the collective view on that occasion was that to be functional in mathematics young people need problem solving skills backed up by appropriate content knowledge. There was a high level of unanimity about this and a rejection of the supposed alternative view that Functional Mathematics was all about routine techniques and algorithms. At the time of writing this paper, development work has yet to begin on turning these ideas into a syllabus with accompanying methods of assessment.

8.4.3 Comparison with Key Skills

In the Tomlinson recommendations, Functional Mathematics was one of seven core components. The complete list is given in Recommendation 6 of the final report.

Three of the items mirror the three main Key Skills.

Tomlinson proposed core	Main Key Skills
Functional Mathematics	Application of Number
Functional Literacy and Communication	Communication
Functional ICT	ICT

The remaining items in the Tomlinson core map less closely to the wider Key Skills individually but collectively form a not dissimilar package.

Tomlinson proposed core	Wider Key Skills
An extended project Common knowledge, skills and attributes Personal review planning and guidance Wider activities	Problem solving Improving own learning and performance Working with others

The similarity with Key Skills is not surprising. Both the 14–19 Working Group and those who devised the Key Skills (and the earlier Core Skills) were responding to the same problem, that of establishing a programme that will allow young people to function more effectively in the adult world.

Similar ideas permeate *Mathematical Skills in the Workplace*[5] where the term 'mathematical literacy' is used. The paragraph which follows is taken from the foreword by the Steering Group.

> *A key finding of this study is that 'mathematical literacy' is displacing basic numeracy as the minimum mathematical competency required in a large and growing number of jobs. Mathematical literacy is the term we have used to describe the application of a range of mathematical concepts integrated with a detailed understanding of the particular workplace context. There is a need to distinguish between numeracy, mathematical skills and mathematical literacy.*

However, the detailed assessment arrangements for the Key Skills, and particularly Application of Number, have not been well received. So it will be important to apply new thinking in the detailed design of Functional Mathematics, including its assessment.

8.4.4 The assessment of Functional Mathematics

The expected relationship between Functional Mathematics and GCSE is defined in Chapter 5 of the White Paper. The two extracts below have already been quoted earlier in this chapter.

> *We will ensure that young people can gain a qualification for achieving the functional skills, even if they are not able to achieve a full GCSE. ... We expect, however, that most students should continue to complete a full GCSE.*

> *We will ensure that no-one can get a C or better in English or maths without mastering the functional elements. Where a young person achieves the functional element only, we will recognise that separately*

In this proposal, Level 2 Functional Mathematics will be part of GCSE1.

It is not possible at this stage, while the meaning of the term 'Functional Mathematics' is still subject to discussion and when no development work has taken place, to be definite about how it will be assessed and how, in detail, this will relate to the assessment of GCSE1. Nonetheless, it is appropriate to explore, speculatively, some issues that might arise.

The assessment system for Functional Mathematics should be simple for all concerned. The more units that are involved the more complicated it becomes for students and teachers, and the more expensive to administer. New schemes have often suffered from excessively complicated assessment regimes.

The implication of the White Paper is that the Functional Mathematics qualification will be awarded as part of the GCSE assessment. That means that if there are problems with the Functional Mathematics part, they will also discredit the whole GCSE and so be even more damaging.

Because it is to be a national qualification, its assessment will be associated with pressure. That makes it difficult to include any internally marked portfolio work or coursework. The assessment criteria for the portfolio work for Application of Number are severely criticised for being so bureaucratic that they distort the work so that it bears little relationship to the skill that it is supposed to be all about. Criteria are necessary to establish uniform standards across institutions, but the question remains open as to whether it is possible to establish a set that will be sufficiently robust for high stakes assessment of the variety of appropriate portfolio work.

In this proposal it is therefore suggested that there should be neither portfolio work nor coursework in the assessment of Functional Mathematics.

A simple model could be to use the on-line test for GCSE1 as the assessment for the whole of the Functional Mathematics qualification but that would depend on the viability of including some aspects of problem solving in that test.

An on-line examination, including the low technology multiple choice format, can be used to test procedural knowledge and simple technical skills. However it can also be used to test the ability to solve problems; the various mathematics challenge papers show how this can be done at a relatively high level. There is no reason why this approach cannot be adapted for lower level unstructured tasks, including comprehension questions.

A related point is that students taking the Functional Mathematics qualification as part of GCSE1 will also be working towards a problem solving paper so their total experience will include working on extended problems in the classroom. This will not, however, be the case of adults taking Skills for Life qualifications, although many of those will have relevant, alternative experience from their employment.

8.5   The relationship between difficulty and uptake

Figure 3 on page 13 shows GCSE1 assessing up to Level 7 of the National Curriculum, GCSE2 up to Level 9. Both of these levels will need careful consideration.

Level 7 is currently achieved by 50% of 16-year-olds. Setting the standard a little lower could increase the number of students who would see it as a reasonable aspiration and so be motivated by it. However, this is not a simple matter both because of the relationship between GCSE1 and the national qualification in Functional Mathematics, and also because the proposed different assessment structure, with one on-line paper, could well yield significantly better results. Furthermore achieving Level 7 does not at present imply mastering Level 7 content, so analogies are difficult to draw.

Further, with two GCSE qualifications available, it is to be hoped that mathematics will receive an increase in teaching time and that would have a significant effect on success rates. There would also be an increase in the numbers taking both GCSE1 and GCSE2 compared to Higher Tier GCSE and there would be a decrease in those who do not progress beyond Level 1 by the age of 16, two years after completing Key Stage 3.

The qualification GCSE2 raises a tension between wanting to make it accessible to perhaps 30–35% of the cohort and providing challenge for the most able. At the moment a significant number of students take Higher Tier GCSE in Year 10 and then either take the Additional Mathematics FSMQ or start on AS modules in Year 11. The White Paper might seem to suggest the latter course of action in paragraph 6.25.

For those who do accelerate, we will make it easier to begin advanced study. Some students may take only one or two units and would be able to bank these towards the achievement of A Levels or a level 3 diploma post-16. Others may take whole AS or equivalent qualifications in Year 11 and their achievement will be recognised in performance tables. ...

However, experience has shown that in mathematics, taking AS modules can create problems, particularly for students who are about to change institutions or those who do not intend to continue with mathematics in Year 12, so that for many Additional Mathematics is now the preferred option. It may prove necessary to provide a similar *'equivalent qualification'* in this new structure; however, it is also possible that the proposed papers involving problem solving and competition type questions will make the Additional Mathematics unnecessary.

Students will also be able to use the extension material currently being developed by QCA in response to Recommendation 4.5 of the Smith report.

8.6   A framework for improved provision

The proposed new framework is a first step towards a solution of the problem, identified in Section 2.1, of making suitable provision for the whole cohort up to the age of 16. It will create the space in which the different needs of students across the ability range can be met.

However, for it to be successful, the various elements designed for this age group, Entry Level Mathematics, Level 1 Mathematics, GCSE1 (including Functional Mathematics) and GCSE2, must engage their target students, including those who currently show little or no interest in mathematics. The authors of this paper have no doubt that this is achievable, given suitable development work, bringing together pedagogy, content and assessment.

9   Take-up post-16

In Chapter 2, three reasons were suggested for the low take-up of Mathematics post-16.

9.1   Students are discouraged by GCSE

The new arrangements at GCSE, including the accompanying changes in pedagogy, will ensure that students entering Year 12 have had a much more positive experience of mathematics and so will be correspondingly more likely to continue with the subject in some form. This will be true whether they have taken GCSE2, with its natural progression route through AS and A Level, or whether they have taken GCSE1 only and so are likely to be progressing through either AM or S1.

The elements A and FM will be much like current AS and A Levels in Mathematics and Further Mathematics and so will draw from a similar pool of students as present courses, although it is anticipated in substantially greater numbers.

9.2   Lack of suitable courses

While the numbers currently taking AS and A Level mathematics could and should be substantially higher, it would be surprising if they were ever to rise to more than about 25% of the age cohort.

The potential for increased numbers is thus greater among the rest of the cohort, those who would benefit from some form of mathematics as a service subject. Some will be taking AS and A Levels in other subjects and others vocational courses.

The target students are those who have completed GCSE1 in Year 11 at the age of 16. Many of these students will only take a single unit of mathematics but others will continue to the equivalent of AS Level or more.

Two routes of progression are proposed, one based on applications of mathematics and the other on statistics. The entry points for these routes are the elements AM and S1, both of which are essentially new although they will draw on the experience gained from existing courses including Free Standing Mathematics Qualifications at levels 2 and 3 and from those mathematics units that are currently available in vocational courses.

The lack of mathematics learnt by vocational students is partly due to the fact that few Advanced VCEs contain mathematics units, but another contributory factor is a lack of enthusiasm for the subject. Thus where optional units are available their uptake is usually low. Consequently awarding bodies are cautious about developing such courses, and schools and colleges are disinclined to deliver them.

There is, however, an underlying philosophical debate about whether the mathematics in vocational courses is better taught in context, as it arises naturally, or in separate units. This issue is not restricted to vocational courses; much the same discussion takes place as to whether statistics should be taught in mathematics or where it occurs in other subjects. The provision proposed in this paper is based on the premise that separate mathematics units may be appropriate to support other courses where two conditions apply.

- The course requires a significant amount of mathematics or statistics, rather than the odd isolated technique.
- Students will benefit from a clear route of progression in mathematics or statistics.

9.2.1 Applicable mathematics

The element AM is designed for those taking numerate courses, such as science and engineering; the courses may be academic or vocational. The target students have taken GCSE1 but not GCSE2. At present, many such students do no mathematics and their progress is consequently limited.

For those who wish to take more mathematics, the route of progression for this element is through AS and A Level Mathematics. However, this element will provide a qualification in its own right.

The first step in increasing the uptake of mathematics among the target students is for schools and colleges to make it generally available. This in turn means that it must be economical for them to provide appropriate courses, such as this element. To make it easier to assemble viable teaching groups, it is proposed that this element should serve a range of numerate courses, rather than have a number of forms, each giving support for a particular course. Ideally it will be used as a unit in several of the 14 specialised learning lines identified in the White Paper in Chapter 7, *A new system of Diplomas*.

9.2.2 Elements S1 and S2

The element S1 will serve a different clientele from AM. The target students will not be doing mathematics but will be doing subjects that require statistics. Examples of such subjects are economics, geography, biology and psychology; indeed all of the sciences and social sciences come into this category. The same is also true for many vocational courses, for example in health and social care. The progression route will be into S2, an extension of S1 into the equivalent of AS Statistics, rather than into AS and A Level Mathematics.

It is widely recognised that statistics is a subject area of key importance. Everyone needs some understanding of how to cope with uncertainty and variability and how to deal with risk. This applies in everyday adult life and in many employment sectors.

Statistics is founded in mathematics, and will continue to be a feature of the mathematics curriculum throughout the levels of the pathways described in this paper, including at AS and A Level, as it is in the present curriculum. However the present post-16 curriculum does not serve those using statistics as a service subject well. They are taking subjects where statistics is used and they need to be able to learn it without being forced to take a mathematics course.

The new S1 and S2 elements will be designed specifically to cater for these students. Although these elements will bear some similarity to the rather limited current provision of GCSE and AS Statistics, they will be much more focused on the needs of the other subjects. Thus the central feature of these units will be to look at the kinds of problems and data that arise in these subjects, and to consider how statistical methods can be used to enhance substantive understanding of the subjects. Mathematics will of course be in the background of this work, but it will not be used for its own sake. The new elements will therefore be much more attractive to students of these other subjects; the courses will be seen as natural supporting material which everyone should know.

It is therefore expected that there will be a larger uptake of statistics post-16 than is currently the case.

9.3 Mathematics is perceived to be harder than other subjects

By providing students with the skills needed for progression, the improved arrangements at GCSE should help to dispel the perception that mathematics is harder than other subjects in Years 12 and 13. This will be brought about by the content of the GCSE courses, particularly the problem solving requirements, and also by much higher grade thresholds on the examination papers. The question of how higher grade thresholds will be achieved is discussed in Section 14.3.1.

In addition, the various courses available in Year 12 will have been designed to follow on from those taken in Year 11. At present many students claim there is a big jump between Years 11 and 12 in mathematics, but this no longer needs to be the case.

10   Looking after the needs of all

A feature of the proposed framework is that the needs of all students are addressed, and not just those towards the middle of the ability range. In mathematics one or two sizes definitely do not fit all. Our national framework must include suitable courses for the whole range of students, including the most talented and those who find the subject most difficult.

10.1 Entry Level and Level 1 provision

Most students will go straight from Key Stage 3 to the element GCSE1.

The Entry Level and Level 1 elements, taken singly or in combination, are designed for those who would find this an unrealistically large step and are consistent with the requirements stated in the final bullet point on page 36 of the White Paper.

> *… we will provide more opportunities and incentives for young people who have not achieved level 2 by 16 to do so post-16 and support them in achieving level 1 or entry level qualifications as steps on the way.*

These elements will contribute towards the new level 1 Diploma described in paragraph 9.12 of the White Paper.

> *The new level 1 Diploma will provide a wholly new opportunity for young people to take qualifications at which they can succeed and which then prepare them to progress to the next level. As a consequence, we expect more young people to attain higher levels, by taking a little longer to get there where necessary. At the same time, the separate identification of the core of functional maths and English and the introduction of level 1 functional skills qualifications into KS4 will ensure that more young people are working at an appropriate level in the basics.*

In highlighting the dual purpose of the level 1 Diploma, as an end in itself and as a way-stage to the level 2 qualifications, the White Paper draws attention, perhaps inadvertently, to the risk that it might come to be regarded as of little value in its own right. That danger will only be overcome if the diploma comes to be appreciated by end-users; those who hold it must be able to carry out certain tasks reliably.

The question of whether these elements will motivate students is discussed in Section 14.1.1.

10.1.1   The Entry Level element

The Entry Level element will provide the Entry Level qualification in mathematics. It will cover Levels 1 to 3 of the current National Curriculum.

The target students for Entry will be in the lowest 10% of the cohort, at age 16 or above, and the course will be designed with such students in mind.

Students working at this level require a flexible and accessible assessment structure, that is '*designed to facilitate learning in practical situations that motivate candidates and that are relevant to adult life*'[12]. Currently the accreditation criteria allow, and indeed encourage, a wide variety of evidence, much of it formative and thus able to support assessment for learning. Suitable use will be made of this flexibility, in contrast to the present situation where '*some awarding bodies… rely heavily on paper-based evidence*' and do not currently '*make full use of the flexibility allowed by the accreditation criteria*'[13].

The assessments that will be developed for the new Entry Level qualification will aim to exploit the full range of types of acceptable evidence, to create the maximum degree of flexibility for students with different special assessment needs. These will include structured practical activities, and the collection of ephemeral evidence that arises naturally in the context of the students' work or training, as well as more formal tests and coursework.

It is possible, but not certain, that some aspects of the assessment may advantageously be delivered on-line. There are dangers in simply transporting written questions into a digital context; the best and most creative written questions could well be lost because the computer cannot cope with the complexities of extended constructed response, while the opportunities for new digital item types are not exploited. Should an item bank be developed for on-line tests for this element, it will need to be composed of questions designed specifically for that purpose.

10.1.2   The Level 1 Mathematics element

As its name suggests, the Level 1 Mathematics element will provide a level 1 qualification.

There will be two target groups of students.

*   Those who have successfully completed the Entry Level qualification and wish to progress further.
*   Those who have not taken the Entry Level qualification but need a realistic way-stage (for example at age 16) on their way to the level 2 Functional Mathematics qualification and GCSE1.

The assessment will be similar to that for Entry Level, with an appropriate balance between the various possible techniques.

This qualification will be at level 1 and so will differ from Foundation Tier GCSE which is a level 2 qualification. The grading will need to reflect this change; thus Pass, Merit and Distinction may be appropriate.

10.2 Talented students

The Smith report highlights concern for the most able students in two of its recommendations. Recommendation 4.5 deals with GCSE.

> *The Inquiry recommends that the QCA and its regulatory partners should be funded to develop an extension curriculum and assessment framework for more able pupils at Key Stages 3 and 4. This extension curriculum should be firmly rooted in the material of the current Programmes of Study, but pupils should be presented with greater challenges. These should involve harder problem solving in non-standard situations, a greater understanding of mathematical inter-connectedness, a greater facility in mathematical reasoning (including proof) and an ability to engage in multi-step reasoning and more open-ended problem solving (see, also, Recommendation 4.11).*

Recommendation 4.10 deals with A Level.

> *The Inquiry recommends that there should be an immediate review by the DfES, LSC and the relevant devolved authorities of measures that could be taken to support and encourage current GCE course provision for the most able mathematics students.*

The framework proposed in this paper provides a clear pathway for the most talented students.

$$\text{Key Stage 3} \rightarrow \text{GCSE1} + \text{GCSE2} \rightarrow \text{A} \rightarrow \text{FM} \rightarrow \text{Higher Education}$$

The content of the various elements, and their methods of assessment, should ensure that at each stage suitable challenges are available for these students. However, the tension between making GCSE2 accessible to a reasonable number of students and meeting the needs of the most able has been noted in Section 8.5, and it may be necessary to provide an extra qualification at this stage, like the present Additional Mathematics FSMQ.

By contrast a wealth of Further Mathematics modules are available to talented students, obviating any need for extra provision at that level.

11   Comparison with the Smith Report

11.1   Comparison with the Smith recommendations

In this chapter the proposed framework is matched to the recommendations and findings contained in Chapter 4 of the Smith Report.

Recommendation 4.1

The Inquiry recommends that, subject to the present pilot being fully and successfully evaluated, immediate consideration be given by the QCA and its regulatory partners to moving as soon as is practicable to a two-tier system of overlapping papers for GCSE Mathematics in England, Wales and Northern Ireland. The Inquiry recommends that the regulatory authorities try to recruit more schools and colleges to take part in pre-implementation piloting after summer 2004.

Recommendation 4.2

The Inquiry recommends that, at the earliest possible opportunity, consideration should be given by the QCA and its regulatory partners to re-designating GCSE Mathematics, appropriately modified if necessary, to merit a double award at level 2. This re-designation should be considered in tandem with the possible move to a two-tier system (see Recommendation 4.1).

The proposed framework combines these two recommendations by making GCSE1 and GCSE2 into the two Subjects in a double award at GCSE; each will have a single tier of entry. The full range of grades will be available for each Subject.

Recommendation 4.3

The Inquiry recommends that there should be an immediate review by the QCA and its regulatory partners of the quantity of coursework in GCSE mathematics and, in particular, the data handling component, with a view to reducing the amount of time spent on this specific element of the course. (See, also, Recommendation 4.4).

This recommendation would be taken into account in the detailed work that would be required in defining the content and assessment instruments for the elements GCSE1 and GCSE2.

Recommendation 4.4

The Inquiry recommends that there should be an immediate review by the QCA and its regulatory partners of the future role and positioning of Statistics and Data Handling within the overall 14–19 curriculum. This should be informed by: (i) a recognition of the need to restore more time to the mathematics curriculum for the reinforcement of core skills, such as fluency in algebra and reasoning about geometrical properties and (ii) a recognition of the key importance of Statistics and Data Handling as a topic in its own right and the desirability of its integration with other subject areas (see, also, Recommendation 4.11).

This recommendation is being acted upon by QCA but it will be some time before the outcomes of the review are known. The proposals in this paper involve the complete redesign of GCSE and so that would provide an opportunity to drop the statistics coursework, which is proving to be very time-consuming at the expense of other parts of the mathematics syllabus.

Recommendation 4.5

The Inquiry recommends that the QCA and its regulatory partners should be funded to develop an extension curriculum and assessment framework for more able pupils at Key Stages 3 and 4. This extension curriculum should be firmly rooted in the material of the current Programmes of Study, but pupils should be presented with greater challenges. These should involve harder problem solving in non-standard situations, a greater understanding of mathematical inter-connectedness, a greater facility in mathematical reasoning (including proof) and an ability to engage in multi-step reasoning and more open-ended problem solving (see, also, Recommendation 4.11).

This recommendation concerns the needs of more able students. It will be taken into account in defining the content, pedagogy and assessment instruments of the element GCSE2.

Recommendation 4.6

The Inquiry recommends that QCA and its regulatory partners undertake a comparative review and make re-designations as necessary, to ensure that claimed equivalences of levels of mathematics qualifications are well founded.

This recommendation will be embedded in the detailed work on the new framework. It is likely to affect elements AM and S1 particularly, ensuring they are set at an appropriate standard.

Recommendation 4.7

The Inquiry recommends that the QCA and its regulatory partners undertake an immediate review of current problems of delivery, content, assessment and availability of courses at levels 1–3 provided by FSMQs, AS Use of Mathematics, AoN and Adult Numeracy. The aim of this review should be to identify scope for improvements in and potential rationalisation of this provision, including opportunities for more systematic integration of ICT in teaching and learning, as part of the longer term design of a new 14–19 pathway structure for mathematics (see also recommendation 4.11).

The framework described in this paper will form part of the *'longer term design'* referred to in this recommendation. Its development will, as a matter of course, take account of the various courses (FSMQs, AS Use of Mathematics, AoN and Adult Numeracy) mentioned, incorporating them into a common post-16 framework. Opportunities for more systematic integration of ICT into teaching and learning are discussed in Section 12.6.

Recommendation 4.8

The Inquiry recommends that the effects of the introduction of the revised specifications for GCE be closely monitored by the QCA and its regulatory partners as a matter of high priority and that funding be made available to support this. If there is no significant restoration of the numbers entering AS and A2 mathematics within the next two or three years, the Inquiry believes the implication for the supply of post-16 qualified mathematics students in England, Wales and Northern Ireland to be so serious that consideration should be given by the DfES and the relevant devolved authorities to offering incentives for students to follow these courses. One possible form of incentive could take the form of financial incentives to HEIs to include AS or A level mathematics as a prerequisite for certain degree courses. Another possibility might be to offer financial incentives directly to students following such courses in HEIs, possibly through fee waivers or targeted bursaries.

QCA are acting on this recommendation. It emphasises the importance of more students taking mathematics post-16. That need is implicit in the proposed framework with its built-in pathways to encourage more students to learn more mathematics at every level.

Recommendation 4.9

The Inquiry recommends that the QCA and its regulatory partners conduct an immediate review of the frequency and style of current GCE assessment, with a view to reducing the time spent on external examinations and preparation for examinations.

The outcomes of this recommendation will be taken into account in defining the assessment instruments for the elements A and FM. This is discussed further in Section 12.3.

Recommendation 4.10

> *The Inquiry recommends that there should be an immediate review by the DfES, LSC and the relevant devolved authorities of measures that could be taken to support and encourage current GCE course provision for the most able mathematics students. In particular, we believe there is a need to ensure that there are no funding disincentives in schools and colleges for providing access to Further Mathematics and the Advanced Extension Award in mathematics. We also believe that consideration should be given to employing the same incentives as suggested in Recommendation 4.8.*

This recommendation is about the needs of the most able mathematics students. The proposed framework will support them by providing an appropriate pathway consisting of elements GCSE1 (taken at an age when they are ready for it), GCSE2, A and FM. The DfES is now funding the Further Mathematics Network[14] to ensure that all students who can benefit from it have access to Further Mathematics.

Recommendation 4.11

> *The Inquiry recommends that funding be provided to the QCA and its regulatory partners to commission, through an open bidding process, up to three curriculum and assessment development studies of variants of these pathway models and approaches, including trialling, feedback and modification and an assessment of the workload implications. These studies should take on board developments arising from Recommendations 4.4, 4.5 and 4.7. The aim of this exercise will be to inform the selection of a preferred pathway model to form part of the reformed 14–19 structure in England and possible parallel developments in Wales and Northern Ireland. Given the importance of ensuring the widest possible involvement and commitment of the mathematics community to the outcome, the Inquiry recommends that the regulatory authorities work in partnership with ACME and mathematics community representatives from Wales and Northern Ireland, and that the DfES and relevant devolved authorities provide appropriate funding to support this.*

This paper is a direct response to this recommendation.

11.2 Comparison with pathways models in the Smith report

The Smith report offers four possible pathways models and these are considered in this Section. None of them meets our needs satisfactorily.

11.2.1   'A possible 14–19 pathways model' in the Smith report

Figure 8, below, is reproduced from the Smith report where it is Figure 4.2.

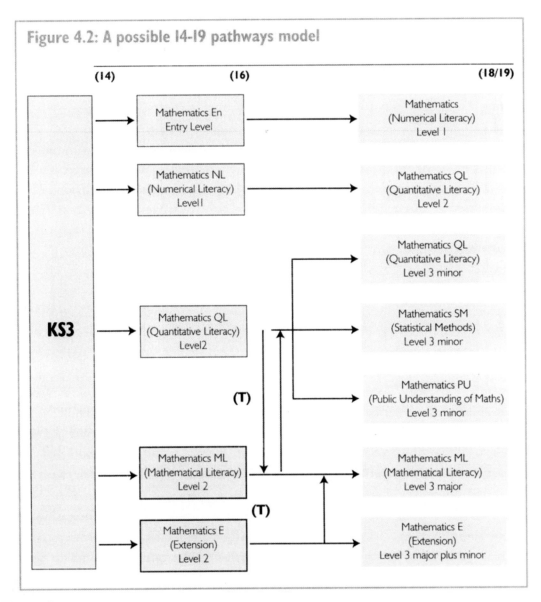

Figure 8

The Entry and Level 1 elements in this paper, and the relationship between them, correspond closely to 'Mathematics En' and 'Mathematics NL' in the Smith pathways diagram.

Thereafter, however, a major inconsistency opens up between the text of the Smith report and the diagram. In paragraph 4.43, the Smith report says

> *... it will be important to avoid regression to old style O level versus CSE, or any other now defunct rigid qualifications divide; ...*

The authors of this paper whole-heartedly endorse that sentiment.

O Level and CSE provided alternative qualifications at what is now termed level 2 and many students were allocated to one or other course at the age of 14. The government of the day claimed the two were equivalent but end-users gave higher status to O Level. Consequently many CSE students suffered from low self-esteem, seeing themselves as second class citizens. Any system which selects children at the age of 14 for courses leading to different level 2 qualifications will produce the same problem. It will also discriminate against late developers.

However, Figure 4.2 in the Smith report illustrates a system in which, from the age of 14, children follow courses aimed at three essentially different level 2 targets: 'Quantitative Literacy', 'Mathematical Literacy' and 'Mathematics Extension'. The problems associated with such a three-way split would be even greater than those encountered in the days of O level and CSE. End-users would soon decide for themselves on the relative values of the three different level 2 qualifications available and public opinion would quickly follow.

That problem is avoided in this proposal. Virtually all students are expected to take both the national qualification in Functional Mathematics and GCSE1.

11.2.2   'A simplified model' in the Smith report

The problem of selection at the age of 14 is also present in two of the remaining three pathways models in the Smith report. The 'simplified model' is illustrated in Figure 4.3 in the Smith report and reproduced overleaf as Figure 9. Children follow one of two pathways at level 2, '*Use of Mathematics*' or '*Mathematics*'. '*Use of Mathematics*' would be the easier route, progressing into a course like the present AS Use of Mathematics. It is entirely predictable that, at level 2, '*Use of Mathematics*' would become the new CSE and '*Mathematics*' the new O Level.

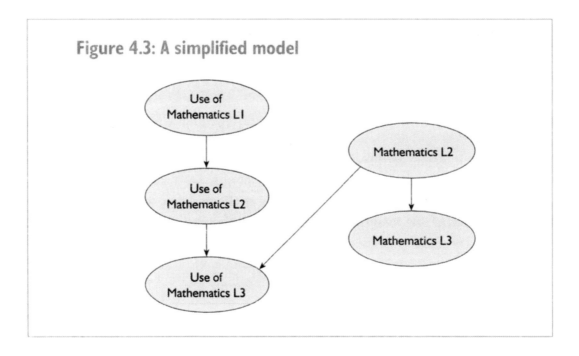

Figure 9

11.2.3   'An alternative pathways model' in the Smith report

The same problem arises with the 'An alternative pathways model', illustrated by Figure 4.4 in the Smith report and reproduced as Figure 10 below.

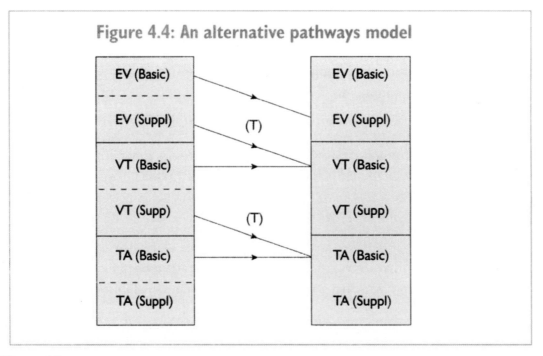

Figure 10

The accompanying text in the Smith report says

> *A … possibility is to develop two or three distinct pathways from a notionally
> accepted common curriculum up to age 14. A version of … this model is shown … in
> Figure 4.4. This proposes three distinct programmes from age 14. These are referred
> to here descriptively as Entry-Vocational (EV), Vocational-Technical (VT) and
> Technical-Academic (TA).*

Again this model reinstates the problems of CSE and O Level, but with a third option
as well.

11.2.4   'The Swedish approach to pathways' in the Smith report

The remaining pathways model in the Smith report is illustrated there as Figure 4.1
and in this paper as Figure 11 below. It illustrates the Swedish model and has the
immediate attraction of avoiding selection at the age of 14. All children set out on a
sequence of elements A, B, C, D, E and they proceed at their own pace, getting as far
as they do during their school careers.

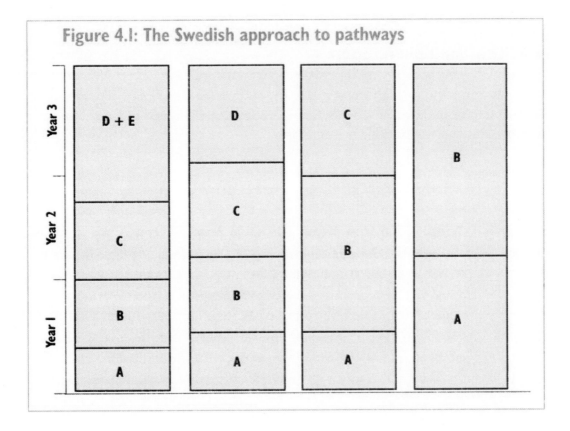

Figure 11

The table below illustrates structural similarities between this model and that proposed in this paper.

This paper	L1	GCSE1	GCSE2	A	FM
Swedish model	A	B	C	D	E

However, there are also important differences.

- The Swedish model covers 3 years rather than 4 and so there cannot be any equivalence of actual content.
- The Swedish model illustrates the last three years of school; everyone is still doing mathematics.
- Everyone is also following a wide curriculum, reducing the need for mathematics courses (like AM, S1 and S2) to support specialised options.

So, although the Swedish model is philosophically close to that proposed in this paper, it is designed to meet the needs of a different overall curriculum.

11.3 The Tomlinson report

The White Paper indicates that changes to the mathematics provision will mostly be based on the Smith report, and work that has been commissioned as a result of its recommendations, for example in paragraph 8.3.

> *Changes to GCSE maths will happen within the context of work already underway in response to Professor Adrian Smith's report, 'Making Mathematics Count'.*

By contrast, those parts of the Tomlinson report which are to be taken forward have been written into the White Paper. Consequently in this paper there is no separate commentary on the Tomlinson recommendations.

Part D: The way ahead

12 How the pathways model supports the White Paper

12.1 Entry Level and Level 1

The model supports the commitment in the White Paper to provide suitable qualifications and pathways for students at Entry Level and Level 1.

In order to do this, Foundation Level GCSE is transformed into a Level 1 qualification. Some improvements are also expected to the Entry Level qualification.

12.2 GCSE

The proposed model involves major changes to GCSE.

In paragraph 8.3, bullet point 2, the White Paper recommends

> *… a review of the content and size of GCSE maths …*

This includes a number of recommendations relating to the structure of GCSE mathematics. The intention is summarised in the next bullet point of paragraph 8.3.

> *It includes development of a curriculum and assessment model for maths provision for setting out clear pathways from National Qualifications Framework (NQF) entry level to level 3.*

The White Paper includes the following major points.

- There is likely to be a new double mathematics GCSE.
- There should be a two-tier GCSE so that no GCSE candidate walks into the examination room knowing that a grade C is impossible.
- There should be a national qualification in Functional Mathematics.

These requirements are all met within the proposed double-award model, with the need for a two-tier GCSE met by two one tier GCSEs.

The qualification in Functional Mathematics is provided as part of the first GCSE in accord with paragraph 8.2 of the White Paper.

It is vital that all young people are able to use English and maths in practice. ...
GCSEs in English and maths should be revised to ensure that students cannot get a
grade C or better without passing (by reaching a high threshold) a functional skills
unit. Those who pass the functional element without succeeding in the GCSE will
have their achievement in the functional unit separately recognised.

Other recommendations for GCSE in the White Paper include reviews of the
provision of statistics and data-handling and of the need for ensuring adequate
provision for gifted students. These are already the subject of work that has been
commissioned by QCA.

12.3   AS and A Level Mathematics

No changes to A Level Mathematics are required immediately by the White Paper.
There are, however, two issues which need consideration.

12.3.1   Number of modules

If paragraph 8.25 of the White Paper were to be taken as applying to mathematics, it
would involve a total rewrite of the Subject Criteria, and completely new
specifications.

Both Sir Mike Tomlinson's 'Inquiry into A level Standards' and the final report of
the Working Group proposed a reduction in the number of assessment units at
A Level without change to their content. We agree. Currently, most A levels have
6 units, each separately assessed and sometimes by more than one exam paper. In
future, most A levels will have four larger units, covering the same amount of
content, but only 4 assessments. This will reduce by a third the assessment burden.
It will also reduce costs and address exam timetabling difficulties. This structure will
not be appropriate in every subject and we expect it to be introduced gradually, as
exams are re-accredited.

The present criteria are based on a ratio of 2:1 between pure and applied
mathematics at both AS and A Level. Changing to 4 units would require this ratio to
become 1:1. This would require a reduction in the pure mathematics content and an
increase in that for applied. This would undo many years of careful work
establishing the present subject core even though it is now widely felt to be
appropriate. If, however, the proposals in GCSE in this paper are accepted, it will be
appropriate to review the approach and content of A Level when, a few years later,
students with new skills start to enter Year 12.

(It should be noted here that unequally weighted units are not a practical proposition
for mathematics. Both the relationship between the single A Level and Further
Mathematics and the need for different pathways through the applied mathematics

make it impossible to design a coherent scheme unless all the units are equally weighted.)

Manifestly such changes would be unsatisfactory in a year when new specifications have just been introduced.

Some six-unit mathematics specifications have been running satisfactorily for nearly 15 years, so there is a strong argument that mathematics is a subject for which the structure will '*not be appropriate*'.

However, there is a case for investigating whether some of the unit assessments could, at a future stage, be carried out on-line, for example that for the first core unit, C1. Almost certainly this could not be done using existing specifications because they have not been designed for such an assessment method. However, it might be possible with some re-allocation of the material between C1 and C2 at AS Level; at A2 Level, a similar redistribution of material between C3 and C4 might allow C3 to be examined on-line. This would reduce somewhat the burden of assessment. However, this is not a course of action to be rushed into and a detailed study would be an appropriate first step.

12.3.2   Extension material

Another possible cause for change is contained in paragraph 8.15.

> *First, we want more stretch within A Levels. Because we make it a priority to preserve A Level as a qualification, with consistent standards over time, we will take a slightly different route to that proposed by the Working Group. We will seek the introduction of a new section in A Level papers covering AEA material. We will ask QCA to consider the best means of doing this across all A levels, so that increased stretch and challenge are available to all students in all types of institutions, and scholarship can flourish.*

While this proposal may fill a general need, mathematics is one subject where this is not the case. Stretch is already present through Further Mathematics, where there is no lack of challenge, particularly at the A2 level. By making AS Further Mathematics more accessible, and by supporting the Further Mathematics Network[14], the government has sent a clear signal of support for Further Mathematics. Now that Further Mathematics is being made accessible to all students who can benefit from it, it would be unhelpful if another form of extension qualification were to be promoted.

If the proposal were to be implemented it would have a major impact on examinations. The papers would need to be longer to fit in the extra questions. (Otherwise easier questions would need to be cut out, making the papers harder and so leading to low grade thresholds.) So, it would increase the burden of assessment.

12.4 Further Mathematics

The White Paper includes a change of policy that could, perhaps unexpectedly, have major implications for Further Mathematics. It is summarised in bullet point 7 on page 60.

At A Level we will enable young people to take HE modules while in the sixth form.

There is considerable overlap between Further Mathematics and parts of the first year work for some university courses. Consequently it ought to be possible to organise syllabuses so that new undergraduates who have done certain Further Mathematics modules are exempted from particular university courses. This would allow them either to move more quickly through university, or to broaden their study with parallel courses.

This idea is not completely new. It was proposed by MEI in the early 1990s and taken up by two universities, Plymouth and John Moore's. However, neither of these universities received many students who had taken Further Mathematics so that uptake was very small.

The environment is rather different now. Further Mathematics will be universally available through the Further Mathematics Network[14] and many more universities recognise the need to engage with the mathematical background of their incoming undergraduates.

It is therefore suggested that a limited study be commissioned to investigate the viability of linking parts of Further Mathematics with early university work, and how such an overlap could be managed by universities. If successful, the study would be used to determine a core for both Further Mathematics and corresponding university courses.

12.5 Other mathematics courses for Year 12 and 13 students

The White Paper says nothing about the mathematical needs of the very large numbers of students who achieve GCSE grade C (or better) at 16 and stay in education but do not choose to take AS or A Level Mathematics. So, in this respect, the proposals made in this paper go beyond the requirements of the White Paper.

12.6   Making use of ICT

Paragraph 8.2, bullet point 2, of the White Paper covers a number of aspects of GCSE mathematics. It includes the following words.

> ... *a review of the role of ICT in the curriculum, teaching and learning, and assessment ...*

The importance of this is highlighted in point 5 of the Executive Summary of *Mathematical Skills in the Workplace*[5].

> *All the sectors exhibit the ubiquitous use of Information Technology. This has changed the nature of the mathematical skills required, while not reducing the need for mathematics. On the contrary, in many cases, a competitive and IT-dependent environment means that many employees are using mathematical skills that their predecessors, or they themselves in the past, did not require.*

12.6.1   ICT in the mathematics curriculum

Today's school students have grown up in the digital age and many are very much at ease with technology. It is even mooted that it has become part of their thinking in a way that is comparable to the facility with languages of children growing up in multilingual societies.

However, so far the impact of technology on the GCSE mathematics curriculum has been at a functional rather than a philosophical level. Calculators have replaced slide rules and logarithm tables, but they are essentially different tools performing much the same tasks.

The proposed changes to the style of GCSE mathematics bring with them the potential for the use of ICT, for example spreadsheets and graphical calculators, as a natural problem solving medium. So it is possible that there will then be changes to what students do rather than to how they do it.

At A Level there have been more significant curriculum changes. Most notably the introduction of statistics was enabled by the advent of calculators. Other curriculum changes in response to ICT are more specification dependent but include numerical methods, advanced matrix work and linear programming, and investigation of curves.

12.6.2   ICT in mathematics learning and teaching

While this paper is, in the first place, about curriculum pathways, these are inextricably linked to good teaching and learning styles. The proposed new GCSE arrangements are designed to ensure that young people emerge with better functional skills so that they can handle real problems with more confidence and greater chance of success. Almost certainly this will involve greater engagement with ICT as a toolkit for the trade.

The authors believe that the new structure will have a major psychological impact on the teaching and learning environment, providing hope to teachers and students who are at the moment denied the prospect of success or of performing to their potential. If this indeed proves to be the case, many teachers will welcome the new beginning with renewed zest for teaching and increased willingness to make use of all the many aspects of ICT.

Students will increasingly be using on-line resources in their own time, including access from home computers and libraries. As well as reinforcing lessons and textbooks, at their best these resources will include animations (to illustrate dynamic processes) and formative assessment instruments.

12.6.3   ICT in mathematics assessment

The proposal includes extensive use of on-line assessment, particular for the two GCSE qualifications and for Functional Mathematics. The possibility of its use in A Level is also raised.

13   Development work needed

The model described in this paper would need considerable development work. This is outlined in the table below.

Element	Level	Work needed
Entry	Entry	Re-design of existing qualification, including part to be Functional Mathematics
L1	1	Design of new qualification, possibly related to the existing Foundation Tier GCSE, part to be Functional Mathematics
GCSE1	2	Design of all aspects of the first part of the new double award GCSE
Fn	2	As a subset of GCSE1, complete design of the new level 2 qualification in Functional Mathematics
GCSE2	2	Design of all aspects of the second part of the new double award GCSE
A	3	A study into the viability of on-line examinations for revised C1 and C3 units
FM	3	A study into the viability of linking parts of Further Mathematics with university courses
AM	2	Design of a route of progression for post-16 students who have completed GCSE1 and are continuing with numerate courses
S1, S2	2 and 3	Design of post-16 statistics-type courses

14   Integrity

A major concern in writing this paper is that it should be possible to translate the model into a mathematics curriculum that will actually work in our schools and colleges. This chapter explores a number of major issues which the authors feel merit serious consideration. Many of the points have already been touched on earlier in the paper; in this chapter they are treated rather more fully.

14.1   Entry Level and Level 1

14.1.1   Will the proposed pathways provide adequate motivation for students working at this level?

The right of all students to access the full 'broad and balanced' curriculum at an appropriate level is now well-established. The model presented in this paper is designed to ensure that such a curriculum is made available.

The key to effective motivation is in the word 'appropriate'. Curriculum and assessment materials for students working at the lower levels, who may have a range of special educational and assessment needs, are sometimes envisaged as just a watered down version of a structure designed for higher-achieving students. This 'top down' approach is rarely effective, and can create a very de-motivating learning environment.

What is proposed here is 'bottom up'. The curriculum would start with the mathematics that is present and relevant in the students' daily life and work, and build on this to develop an understanding of, and an ability to apply, mathematical concepts.

The full range of methods of recording and assessment would be exploited to ensure that the qualifications at Entry Level and Level 1 would be accessible, valid and suitable for the wide range of students for whom they are intended.

14.2   Acceleration

14.2.1   Will a move away from age-related qualifications mean that some students are pushed too far too fast?

While it is clearly the intention of the White Paper that students should not be held back by age related examinations, particularly at 16, there is considerable anxiety among teachers that taking examinations too early will be detrimental to students' long term interests. There are those who would regard 'acceleration' as a swear word.

The term 'acceleration' is actually used in two quite different ways.

- It is sometimes applied to any situation in which a student does work, or takes an examination, at an earlier than 'normal' age; 'normal' usually refers to the median for the cohort. In this usage, students who take GCSE Mathematics at the end of Year 10 have been accelerated, whatever their ability.
- At other times it is applied to a situation in which a student does work that requires faster mental development than is natural for that student. In this case those who take GCSE Mathematics at the end of Year 10 may, or may not, be accelerated; it depends on individual levels and rates of development.

In this section different situations are considered which can be described as acceleration, according to the sense in which the word is being used.

When determining an appropriate national mathematics provision, it is essential that proper account is taken of the full range of mathematical ability among young people. The issues relating to acceleration, or early entry, are usually associated with the more able students.

There have always been, and will always be, children who develop very early in mathematics, including, for example, those who reach degree standard while still at school. To deny such children the right to exercise their talents would be a form of cruelty.

(However, children should remain in their school age groups for their other subjects; one of the authors of this paper went through secondary school in a class with students two to three years older and describes the experience as follows "*I was not allowed to be my own age at school; an important part of my childhood and adolescence was taken away from me, albeit from the best of motives. Child abuse is too strong a term but it was not that far away from it.*")

Such children form the extreme tail of a continuous distribution that includes many who are well above the standard of most of their fellow students in mathematics, and it is often an unhappy experience for them; they can become bored and disruptive in class. The mathematics curriculum must take account of the needs of such children. It should embrace their talents rather than turn them into problem students. If that involves taking examinations at an earlier age than others, so be it.

However, it would be unfortunate if such students' mathematical experience was confined to examination syllabuses; they should for example be encouraged to take part in the enrichment activities offered by The National Academy for Gifted and Talented Youth, to attend master classes and so on.

There are other children for whom acceleration does not provide a positive experience, either because they are towards the middle of the ability distribution or because they are accelerated too fast, for example Year 6 children taking Intermediate Tier GCSE Mathematics and obtaining grade C. Such children often end up with deeply held misconceptions. There are topics which they believe they understand but in reality do not; they can become almost unteachable.

A student's best interest must always be paramount in any decision regarding possible acceleration. Essentially 'acceleration' should not be acceleration at all but allowing the student's natural development to take its course. Here are two tests that might be found helpful when the decision is made and at subsequent reviews.

- Will the student be working at his/her own pace and not under undue pressure?
- Will the student have a realistic prospect of obtaining very high marks in any examinations?

The most common form of 'acceleration' in the pathways proposed in this paper would almost certainly involve students taking GCSE1 at the age of 14. Under the proposed design GCSE1 will test up to Level 7 of the National Curriculum, and Figure 1 on page 10 shows that 25% of 14-year-olds have reached that level. So for such students there would be no acceleration; they would be taking an assessment at the level at which they were working anyway.

If the proposals in this paper are adopted, care will need to be taken in formulating policy over performance tables at Key Stage 3. If, for example, a grade C in GCSE1 were to enhance a school's measure at this point, there would be a conflict of interest between schools and their students.

A final point on this subject is that this pathways design does not compel a school to enter students 'early' for GCSE1 even if they are ready for it. Other patterns of entry are possible, for example taking both GCSE1 and GCSE2 together at the age of 16.

14.3   Assessment for mastery

14.3.1   How can higher grade thresholds become a reality?

There is a marked contrast between grade thresholds at A Level and at GCSE.

For AS and A Level units, papers are typically designed to give raw mark thresholds of 80% for grade A and 40% for grade E. The actual thresholds are set by an awarding committee and some variation from the design is expected; however, it is unusual for such variation to be more than a few marks, and so high thresholds are a feature of A Level grading. That is in stark contrast to GCSE where very low thresholds are common.

The reason for the contrast lies in the different meanings attached to the grades. At A Level marks are designated according to the difficulty of the demand but not the actual content so that the same topic can attract marks at any grade from E to A.

That is not the case at GCSE where there is a much closer relationship between content and grades. This happens because of the association of GCSE grades with National Curriculum Levels, as shown in the table below. Each National Curriculum Level covers specific content.

GCSE grade	G	F	E	D	C	B	A	A*
N.C. Level	4	5	6–7			8	9	10

So an examiner setting a paper covering grades C to A* must include work from Levels 7, 8, 9 and 10. When it comes to the award, grade C must be based on the Level 7 work and this might be as little as one quarter of the paper. Thresholds are typically set at about 80% of the accessible marks for any grade, and so, in this example, the design threshold for grade C would be 80% of ¼, or 20%. If, when the paper is sat for real, the Level 7 questions turn out to have been a bit hard the grade C threshold will end up even lower.

Thus low thresholds are not an accident but a consequence of the way the present mathematics GCSE is designed.

The proposed new double award GCSE will overcome these problems. The syllabuses for both parts will be more tightly defined, each covering about two National Curriculum Levels. This will allow the assessment to be based on the assumption that any candidate has covered the whole of the syllabus, and so differentiation and grading will be based on the difficulty of the demands rather than the National Curriculum Level of a question.

Consequently it will indeed be possible to design high thresholds into papers, as it is at A Level.

14.4   Delivery

14.4.1   Will schools be able to handle students taking examinations when ready?

A free-for-all of examinations on demand could prove very difficult for schools to administer, not least where students are likely to transfer between institutions. The examples in this paper are all based around assessment ages of 14 (for some), 16 and 18–19. It may be that for pragmatic reasons some such restriction will be found appropriate.

14.4.2   Will some students give up mathematics early?

The design has the potential danger of bright students taking the first GCSE, GCSE1, at the age of 14 and then dropping mathematics. However the statutory requirements for those aged 14–16 will still apply, so that mathematics will continue to be compulsory until the age of 16, ensuring that this cannot happen.

A related concern is that, having taken GCSE1 at the age of 14, some schools might direct students, who are obviously of high ability, on to Statistics 1 or Applicable Mathematics rather than the appropriate route of progression, GCSE2. To avoid that happening Statistics 1 and Applicable Mathematics have been designated as post-16 elements.

14.4.3   How can you ensure that talented students working on GCSE1 are sufficiently stimulated?

The problem solving emphasis in GCSE1 will ensure that a substantial amount of the work is open-ended, allowing talented students to follow their own lines of enquiry. In addition some schools may choose to do some teaching for GCSE2 alongside that for GCSE1, as indicated in Figure 7 on page 26, and the syllabuses of the two GCSE qualifications will be designed to allow this to happen.

14.4.4   How will teachers handle this new curriculum?

The curriculum seeks to give considerable emphasis to using content knowledge in the context of solving problems which would be presented in an unstructured format. This requires a substantial change in teaching approaches which maintain a long-standing emphasis on rote learning with constant practice based on standard procedures. Substantial Continuing Professional Development (CPD) at all levels from Key Stage 1 onwards will be required to encourage teachers to embed the learning of techniques in a much more problem centred approach to learning mathematics

Conclusion

During the last two decades, our school mathematics curriculum has been subject to frequent changes, particularly at GCSE.

Any change can be expected to cause some initial difficulties, particularly for the students in its first year, but it is hoped that these will soon be outweighed by obvious improvements. Sadly, the benefits which recent changes were intended to bring have not, on the whole, materialised.

The reason for this lack of success is that many of the recent changes have not been based on a sufficient analysis of the underlying problems. They have been designed to treat the symptoms rather than the disease. The authors believe that they have avoided that mistake in this paper.

The source of our problems lies in the fact that we are no longer seeking to educate a small and talented section of the population but the whole of it. Even though it is now many years since the Raising of the School Leaving Age, we have yet to make appropriate provision for everyone at the age of 16 and the same problem is increasingly repeated at 18 as the numbers staying on edge up towards 100%.

The pathways recommended in this paper are designed to meet the learning and progression needs of the diverse group of young people who make up any age cohort. It is the authors' belief that these proposals, if carefully developed and implemented, would result in a very significant improvement in the standard of mathematics in this country.

Appendix: Problem solving

Problem solving is mentioned in many places in this paper. Although the proposed pathways could be implemented without it, the authors believe that appropriate emphasis on problem solving will ensure that even better learning takes place. In the next two sections, authors with particular expertise in this area write about it.

The first section is a case study, looking at the approaches to problem solving in England and the Netherlands (where it forms the basis of delivery for much of the curriculum). This section draws on the experience of Manchester Metropolitan University in working with materials developed at the Freudenthal Institute[11].

The second section establishes a pedagogical framework to ensure that students really do learn from problem solving. It is based on the experience of the NRICH Mathematics Project[15].

Case study: Is mathematical development supported through a problem solving curriculum?

Currently mathematics teaching has two approaches to utilising realistic situations.

1   Introduce a concept using a context, move quickly to considering the topic abstractly and finally, once a concept or procedure has been learnt, consider applications. This process is illustrated below in Figure 12.

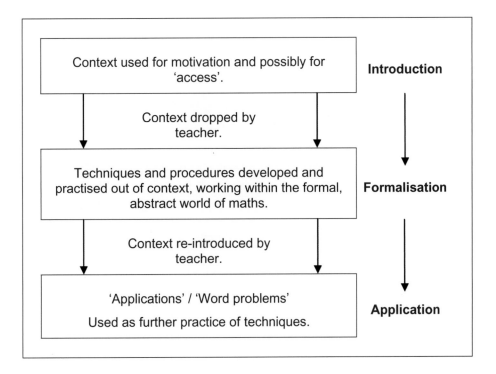

Figure 12: Typical English scheme

This is exemplified by the following advice given to teachers on page 20 of the National Strategy guidelines[16].

> *You can introduce problem solving, applications of mathematics and the use of reasoning and thinking skills at many points in a unit of work. A problem can serve as an introduction, to assess pupils' prior knowledge or to set a context for the work; it can be used to provide motivation for acquiring a skill; or it can be set as a class activity or as homework towards the end of a topic, so that pupils use and apply the mathematics they have been taught.*

2   Use additional materials, such as GAIM or coursework type materials, as enrichment to the normal curriculum.

Research has shown that neither approach has been particularly successful in getting students to work fluently or mathematically in realistic situations[17, 18, 19]. A common response to problems is for students to revert to naïve mathematics or to use algorithms inappropriately.

An approach to teaching developed in the Netherlands called Realistic Mathematics Education (RME) utilises a very different strategy both for the teaching of mathematics and for the development of problem solving skills. Students are provided with realistic problems similar to the original situations within which the mathematical concept was developed and used. Through this device, they are asked to reinvent the mathematics and gradually, over time, to make the mathematics more sophisticated.

Hence contexts are used not only to illustrate the applicability and relevance of mathematics in real world situations, but also as a source for the learning of mathematics itself. They are chosen so as to be experientially real to students, and students are encouraged to make sense of them using their experiences, intuitions and common sense. Students then stay in context, and remain at a sense-making level, while they develop mathematically. The well-evidenced argument is that, through staying connected with the context, students are able to continue to make sense of what they are doing, and do not need to resort to the memorising of meaningless rules and procedures. 'Mathematics' and 'context' are never separated; to experience success in one implies success in the other. The contexts used are extensively researched and differ significantly from those found in standard English textbooks. For example,

• They make much greater use of 'real data' and 'unclean' numbers. Hence estimation, a crucial 'real world' skill, plays a much more prominent part.
• They regularly contain scope not only for different solution strategies, but also for different solutions. There will often be more information than is required, and occasionally not enough.

In these respects, and in others, they are much more akin to real world problems. RME, however, provides a different view not only on how contexts should be chosen, but also on how these can then be used to support mathematical development.

Fundamentally, in England, student development is categorised in terms of procedural and algorithmic knowledge, whereas in Holland educators provide a rich description of development including the use of models, mathematical landmarks, procedures, insights and reflection to inform curriculum designers and teachers[20, 21]. Teachers and educators in England currently trialling this approach are very impressed by student engagement in the mathematics and by the students' conceptual development.

It is important to realise that a fundamental tenet of RME is to build sophistication into student-generated procedures rather than for teachers to impose an algorithm. The research of Anghileri[17] and of Webb[22] attests to the effectiveness of this approach. The table below, adapted from Anghileri, provides an interesting summary of research into student development of division strategies in England and Holland in Year 4.

| | English | | | | Dutch | | | |
| | Test 1 | | Test 2 | | Test 1 | | Test 2 | |
Strategy	Attempt	Correct	Attempt	Correct	Attempt	Correct	Attempt	Correct
Repeated use of divisor	17%	7%	11%	6%	10%	4%	1%	1%
Partitioning (inappropriate)	5%	0%	3%	0%	7%	1%	6%	2%
Low level chunking	6%	2%	8%	2%	16%	7%	6%	5%
High level chunking	8%	5%	7%	5%	41%	28%	69%	51%
Algorithm	38%	18%	49%	25%	4%	1%	3%	1%
Mental (answer only)	9%	5%	11%	6%	9%	6%	11%	7%
Wrong operation	3%	0%	2%	0%	5%	0%	1%	0%
Unclear	4%	1%	3%	0%	2%	0%	1%	0%
No attempt	9%	0%	8%	0%	8%	0%	2%	0%
Total	100%	38%	100%	44%	100%	47%	100%	68%

This and other comparative data show Dutch students being much more adept at solving 'standard problems' than their English counterparts. Dutch students do seem to make short-term gains, but there is a much stronger sense that mastery develops over time, and that fluency has to go hand in hand with understanding. Indeed, it could be argued that fluency replacing understanding, quite typical of English students, is one of the biggest barriers to the development of students as effective problem solvers.

Experience also suggests, however, that moving from an 'applications' model to a genuine context-rich problem-solving model requires significant shifts in teachers' practice and beliefs. While evidence from both US and England suggests that such shifts are possible, these require pedagogical training. This is not just about structural change, where it could be argued that NNS has been most successful, but about changing the habits that shape classroom behaviour on a day-to-day basis.

In summary there is evidence that a curriculum can be created around the notions of problem solving, and that this curriculum can build on our current approaches as long as there is investment in staff and material development. Finally, the available evidence to date would suggest that this type of curriculum supports and enhances students' mathematical development.

Problem solving and mathematical thinking

There is evidence that with the present curriculum many students lack motivation, with consequent dips in their performance; they are being turned off mathematics and fewer students are choosing to study mathematics and mathematics-related subjects beyond the age of 16.

The experience of most students 'doing mathematics' involves studying materials and working through tasks set by others[23] with very little room for the entrepreneur or creative thinker. However, much of mathematics in the real world requires its application to problems to which, by definition, we do not know the answer. The notion of being lost and having to find your way is rarely present in mathematics classrooms but more truly reflects the spirit of mathematics. We do not give students the opportunity, in Schoenfeld's words, to experience

> *The joy of confronting a new situation and trying to make sense of it – the joy of banging your head against a mathematical wall, and then discovering that there may be ways of either going around or over that wall[24].*

However, to achieve this it is necessary to make explicit the content and nature of the skills, knowledge and classroom experience and identify the methodologies for implementation of such an approach. What do the curriculum resources and learning tools look like that help students come to 'know' in this way?

Terms such as 'mathematical thinking', 'mathematical problem solving' and 'enrichment' are variously described in current literature. There, 'enrichment' is used almost exclusively in the context of provision for the mathematically most able. However, there is strong evidence that problems which offer suitable entry points can be used with students of a wide range of ability and therefore can be used within the 'ordinary' classroom. The teacher or mentor can use such materials in flexible ways that respond to the needs (and experience) of the learner. Good mathematics education should incorporate an approach that is enriching and stimulating for all students. The construction of such an approach would build on two main strands.

- Content opportunities designed to
  - develop and use problem solving strategies
  - encourage mathematical thinking
  - include historical and cultural contexts
  - offer opportunities for mathematical extension.
- Teaching that offers opportunities such as
  - group work, discussion, communicating, …
  - varied solutions and different approaches being valued and utilised
  - exploration, making mathematical connections, extending boundaries, celebrating ideas not simply answers, flexibility, …

A range of literature exists in the areas of problem solving and mathematical thinking including the work of Mayer[25], Boaler[26], Schoenfeld[24], Mason et al[27] and Polya[28]. We need to develop abilities in these areas.

The aim is to identify problems where such strategies are useful and create a curriculum that encourages students to develop each strategy and identify the type of context and the ways in which such strategies can be fruitfully employed.

References and notes

1. *14–19 Education and Skills*, Government White Paper, 2005

2. Report of the *Post-14 Mathematics Inquiry*, Chair Professor Adrian Smith, 2004

3. Interim report of the *Working Group on 14–19 Reform*, Chair Mike Tomlinson, 2004

4. *14–19 Curriculum and Qualifications Reform*, Chair Mike Tomlinson, 2004

5. *Mathematical Skills in the Workplace*, Hoyles C., Wolf A., Molyneux-Hodgson S. and Kent P., 2002

6. *Developing a model to describe the progress of secondary school students: findings of the Graded Assessment in Mathematics project*, Brown M., Proceedings of the 10th International Conference on Mathematics Education, 1986

7. Further information on Asset languages may be found at *www.ocr.org.uk*.

8. Key Stage 3 results for 2003, DfES

9. GCSE Results for 2003, JCGQ

10.

GCSE grade	A*	A	B	C	D	E	F	G
N.C. Level	10	9	8	7–6			5	4

11. Further information on the *Mathematics in Context* materials may be found at *www.mic.brittannica.com/mic/common/home.asp*.

12. *Criteria for the Accreditation of External Qualifications – Entry level*, QCA

13. *Evaluation of Entry Level Qualifications*, QCA, ACCAC, CCEA and LSC, 2004

14. Further information on the Further Mathematics Network may be found at *www.fmnetwork.org.uk*.

15. Further information on the NRICH Mathematics Project may be found at *www.nrich.maths.org.uk*.

16. *Key Stage 3 National Strategy for Mathematics*, DfEE, 2001

17. *From informal strategies to structured procedures: mind the gap*, Anghileri J., Beishuizen, M. and van Putten, K., Educational studies in mathematics 49,(2), 2002.

18. *National Numeracy: a brief exploration*, Eade F. and Dickinson P., Mathematics Education Review, 2005

19. Misailidou C. and Williams J. (2003): Proceedings of the 27th Conference of the International Group for the Psychology of Mathematics Education, 2003

20. *Young mathematicians at work*, Fosnot, C.T. and Dolk, M., Heinemann, 2002.

21. *Children learn mathematics*, van den Heuvel-Panhuizen, M., Freudenthal Institute and University of Utrecht, 2001

22. *Summary report of student achievement data for Mathematics in Context*, Webb, D.C. and Meyer, M.R., Holt, Rinehart and Winston, 2002

23. *A discussion of Bruce Reznick's Chapter [Some Thoughts on Writing for the Putnam]*, Olkin, I. and Schoenfeld, A.H., Mathematical Thinking and Problem Solving (Editor Lawrence Erlbaum), 1994

24. *Reflections on doing and teaching mathematics*, Schoenfeld, A.H., Mathematical Thinking and Problem Solving (Editor Lawrence Erlbaum), 1994

25. *Mathematical Problem Solving*, Mayer R.E., Mathematical Cognition (Editor Royer, J.M.), 2002

26. *Experiencing school mathematics – teaching styles, sex and setting*, Boaler, J., Oxford University Press, 1997

27. *Thinking Mathematically*, Mason, J., Burton, L., Stacey, K., Prentice Hall, 1985

28. *How to solve it*, Polya, G., Princeton University Press, 1945

29.   A standard growth chart for girls aged 5 to 18

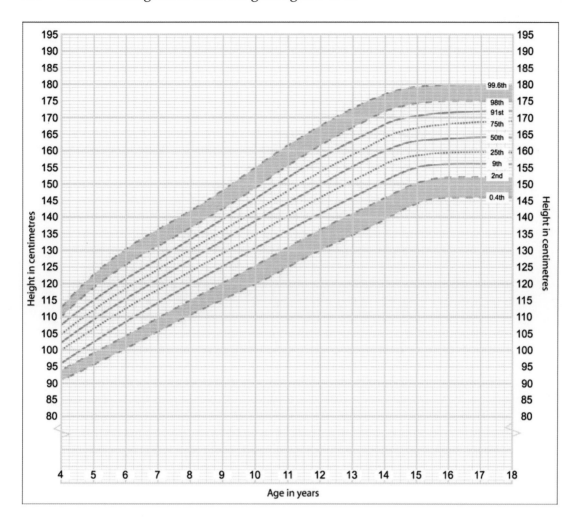